Politics of Culture

A study of three Kirata communities in the eastern Himalayas

T. B. SUBBA

Orient Longman

ORIENT LONGMAN LIMITED

Registered Office
3-6-272 Himayatnagar, Hyderabad 500 029 (A.P.), India

Other Offices
Bangalore / Bhopal / Bhubaneshwar / Chandigarh
Chennai / Ernakulam / Guwahati / Hyderabad / Jaipur
Kolkatta / Lucknow / Mumbai / New Delhi / Patna

First published 1999
Reprint 2001
ISBN 81 250 16937

Typeset in Times Roman by
OSDATA, Hyderabad 500 029

Printed in India at
Sekar Offset, Chennai-5.

Published by
Orient Longman Limited
160, Anna Salai, Chennai 600 002.

The maps in this book are not to scale. The external boundary of India as depicted is neither correct nor authentic.

Dedicated
to
the scientific spirit of
Homi J. Bhabha
and
to my teacher
Professor N. C. Choudhury

Contents

Maps and Tables

Maps

Tables

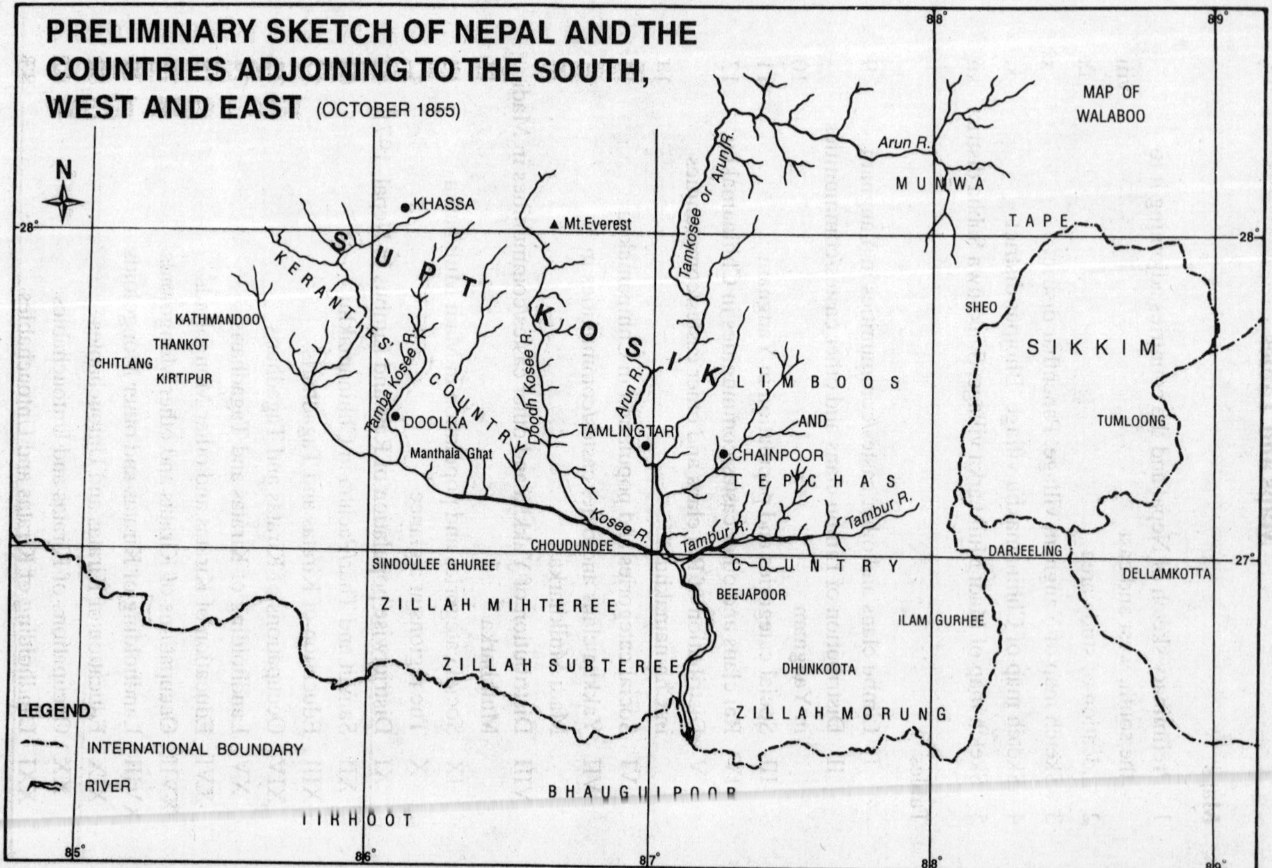

PRELIMINARY SKETCH OF NEPAL AND THE COUNTRIES ADJOINING TO THE SOUTH, WEST AND EAST (OCTOBER 1855)

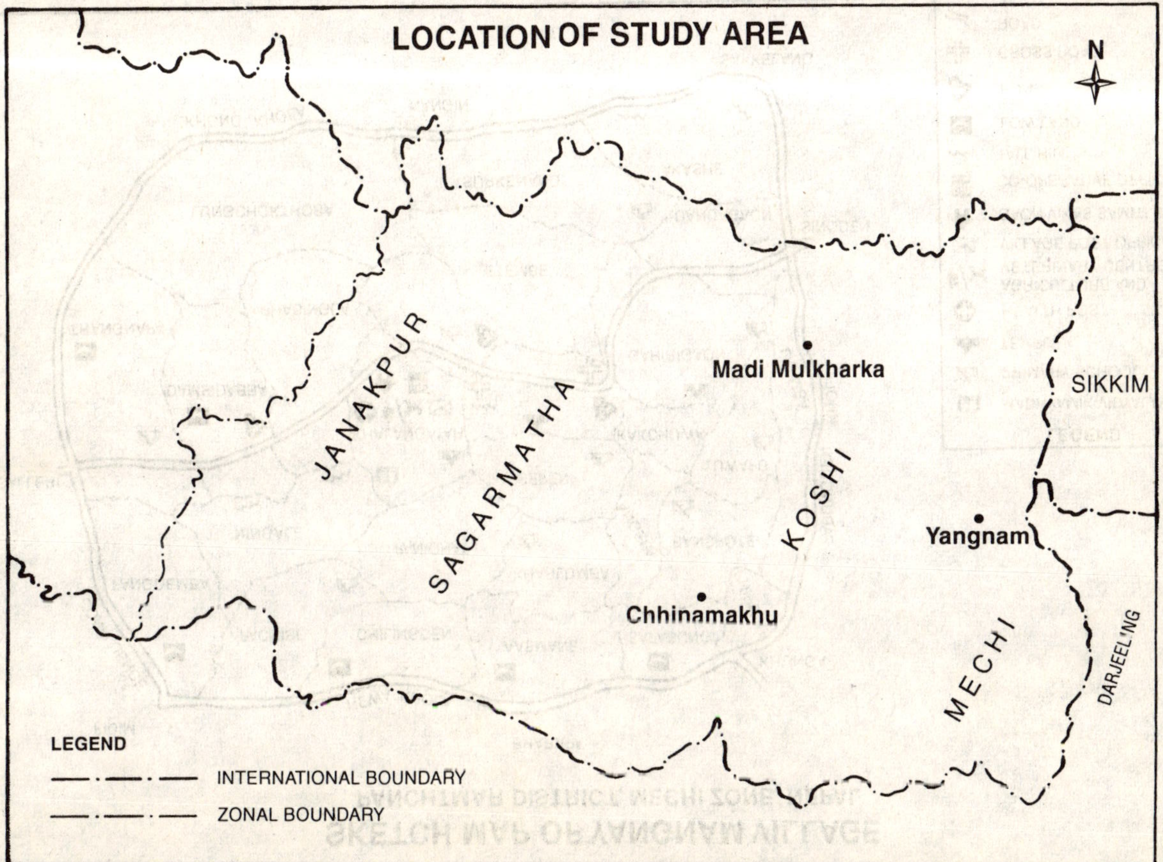
LOCATION OF STUDY AREA
N
SIKKIM
Madi Mulkharka
JANAKPUR
SAGARMATHA
KOSHI
Yangnam
Chhinamakhu
MECHI
DARJEEL'NG
LEGEND
INTERNATIONAL BOUNDARY
ZONAL BOUNDARY

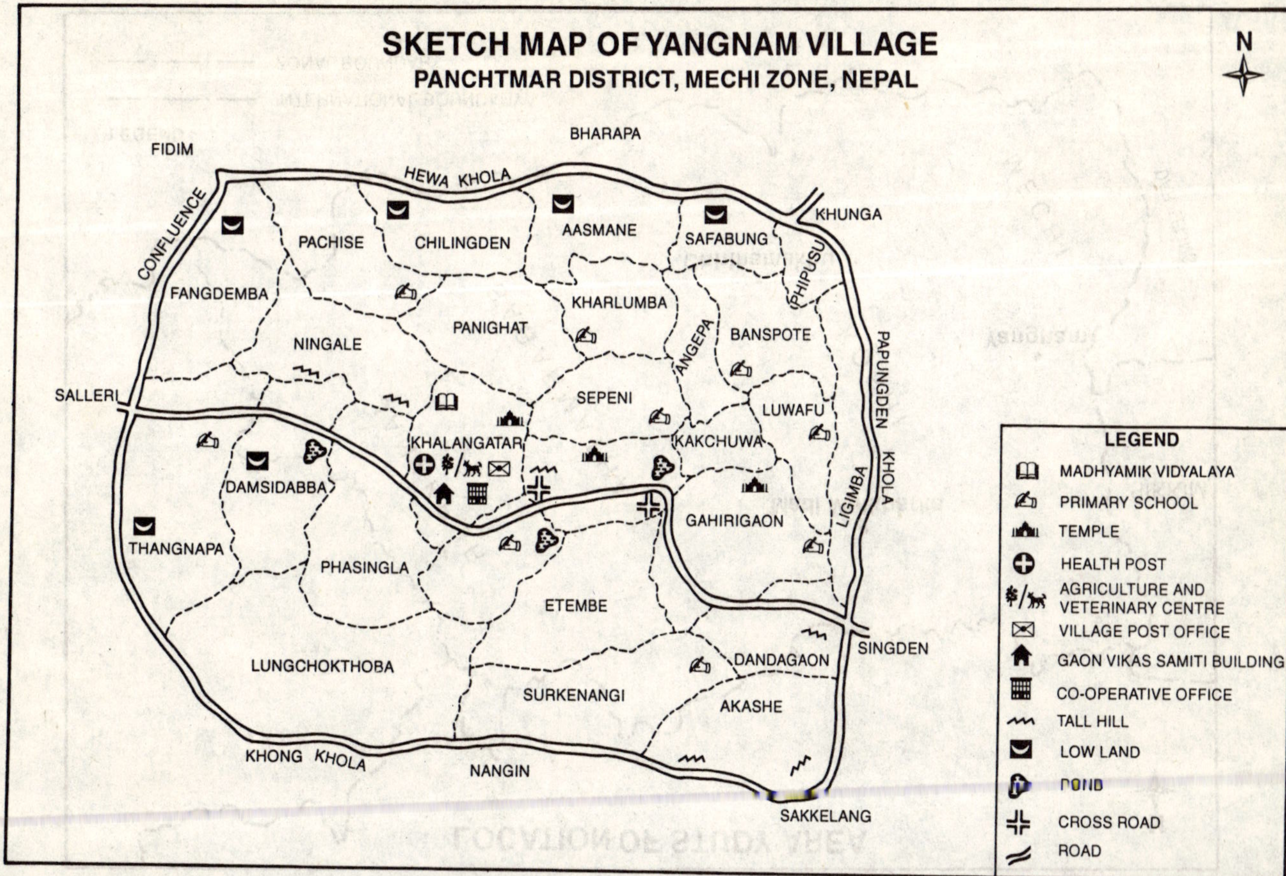
SKETCH MAP OF YANGNAM VILLAGE
PANCHTMAR DISTRICT, MECHI ZONE, NEPAL
N
BHARAPA
FIDIM
HEWA KHOLA
KHUNGA
CONFLUENCE
PACHISE
CHILINGDEN
AASMANE
SAFABUNG
PHIPUSU
FANGDEMBA
KHARLUMBA
PANIGHAT
NINGALE
ANGEPA
BANSPOTE
PAPUNGDEN KHOLA
SALLERI
SEPENI
LUWAFU
KHALANGATAR
KAKCHUWA
DAMSIDABBA
LIGIMBA
THANGNAPA
GAHIRIGAON
PHASINGLA
ETEMBE
SINGDEN
LUNGCHOKTHOBA
DANDAGAON
SURKENANGI
AKASHE
KHONG KHOLA
NANGIN
SAKKELANG
LEGEND
MADHYAMIK VIDYALAYA
PRIMARY SCHOOL
TEMPLE
HEALTH POST
AGRICULTURE AND VETERINARY CENTRE
VILLAGE POST OFFICE
GAON VIKAS SAMITI BUILDING
CO-OPERATIVE OFFICE
TALL HILL
LOW LAND
POND
CROSS ROAD
ROAD

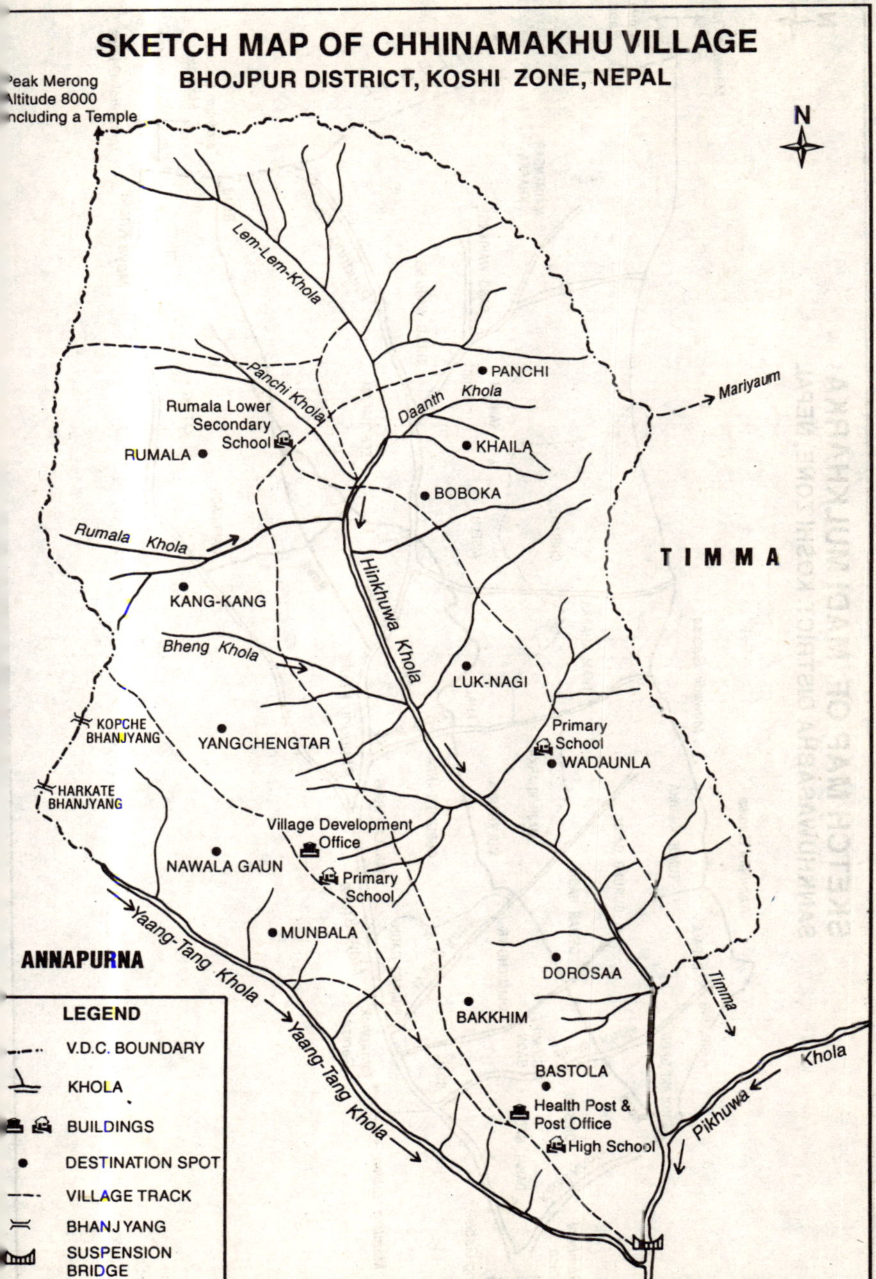
SKETCH MAP OF CHHINAMAKHU VILLAGE
BHOJPUR DISTRICT, KOSHI ZONE, NEPAL
Peak Merong
Altitude 8000
Including a Temple
N
Lem-Lem-Khola
Panchi Khola
PANCHI
Daanth Khola
Mariyaum
Rumala Lower Secondary School
RUMALA
KHAILA
BOBOKA
Rumala Khola
TIMMA
KANG-KANG
Hinkhuwa Khola
Bheng Khola
LUK-NAGI
KOPCHE BHANJYANG
YANGCHENGTAR
Primary School
WADAUNLA
HARKATE BHANJYANG
Village Development Office
NAWALA GAUN
Primary School
MUNBALA
DOROSAA
ANNAPURNA
Yaang-Tang Khola
Timma
BAKKHIM
Yaang-Tang Khola
BASTOLA
Khola
Pikhuwa
Health Post & Post Office
High School
LEGEND
V.D.C. BOUNDARY
KHOLA
BUILDINGS
DESTINATION SPOT
VILLAGE TRACK
BHANJYANG
SUSPENSION BRIDGE

SKETCH MAP OF MADI MULKHARKA
SANKHUWASABHA DISTRICT, KOSHI ZONE, NEPAL

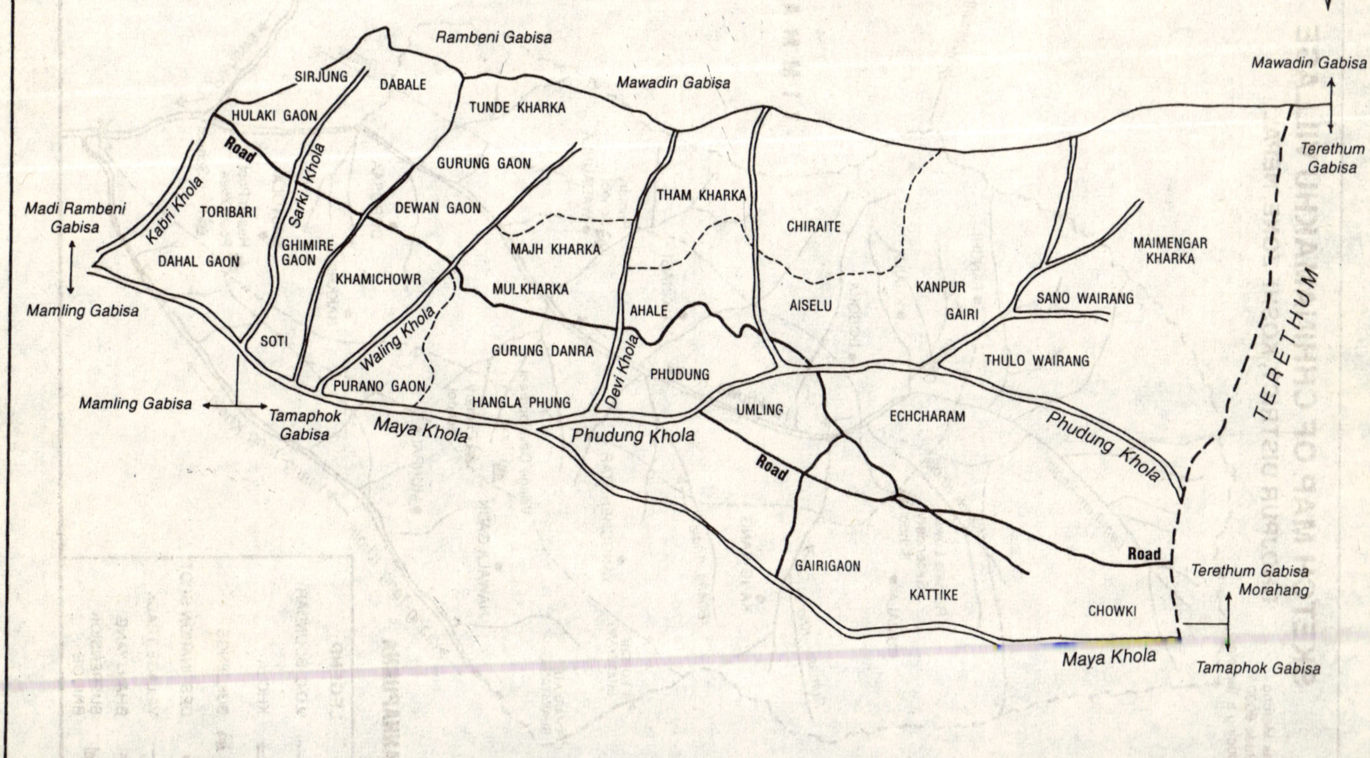

Acknowledgements

My interest in the study of the Kiratas developed about two decades ago when I was doing my doctoral research on the Nepali society of Darjeeling and Sikkim. Later, I was encouraged to take up this study by various scholars like Professor S. K. Chaube, Dr. Michael Aris, Dr. R. Keith Sprigg and the Hon'ble N. Wangchuk. But for different reasons the interest never got translated into action. Efforts were made to get financial support from the Indian Council of Social Science Research and the University Grants Commission in New Delhi but they proved to be rather frustrating. I had almost given up the idea when Professor B. K. RoyBurman suggested that I apply for the Homi Bhabha Fellowship. Fortunately, I was awarded it and here is the work I did for two years of my tenure as a Homi Bhabha Fellow (1 January 1992 to 30 December 1993). I am most grateful to Professor RoyBurman for this and to the Homi Bhabha Fellowships Council in Bombay for giving me this honour. I am particularly grateful to its Assistant Director, Mr H. D. Pajnigar, for taking a personal interest in my work.

This book would not have been possible without the help of a lot of friends. Among them, I have the pleasure of especially mentioning the help of Dr. Prem Po'dar of the English Department, University of Aarhus, Denmark and Benqt G. Karlsson (Beppe) of Uppsala University, Sweden.

I am also indebted to the villagers of Yangnam, Chhinamakhu and Madi Mulkharka, who made my stay in their villages both memorable and educative. I should express my deep gratitude to the following in particular: Hang Oja Jabegou of Yangnam, Surendra Rai and Kala Prasad Rai of Chhinamakhu, and Bhaktamani Dewan and Man Bahadur Majiya of Madi Mulkharka, for many instances of guidance and hospitality.

In Kathmandu, I was helped by a large number of people. I cannot possibly name them all here. But I should acknowledge the help of Kanak

Mani Dixit (Editor, *Himal*), Dr. V. B. S. Kansakar (Centre for Economic Development and Administration), Professor Gopal Singh Nepali (Tribhuwan University), Dr Dilli Ram Dahal (Centre for Nepal and Asian Studies) and Mahesh C. Regmi, who needs no introduction. I am also grateful to the staff of Tribhuwan University library, National Library, National Archives and the Documentation Cell of the Centre for Nepal and Asian Studies.

In Sikkim, I am specially grateful to the following persons: Jigme N. Kazi, S. R. Khajum, B. B. Muringla, T. D. Rai and Michael Pradhan. In Darjeeling, Ms. Surya Kumari Chemjong and Papohang Laxman Lawati were very kind. And in Kalimpong, I am most grateful to my schoolteacher, Khagendra Songpangphe, and to Dr. R. Keith Sprigg, formerly of the School of Oriental and African Studies (SOAS), London.

I must now express my gratitude to the staff of the India Office Library, School of Oriental and African Studies library, Bodleian library, and the library of the Institute of Development Studies at Sussex. I am also grateful to Professor Lionel Caplan and Dr. Michael Hutt at the SOAS, Drs Andrew Russell and Tamara Kohn of Durham University, Dr. Nick J. Allen of Oxford University and Tamara Hudec of Pennsylvania University for helping me in my research work there.

I take this opportunity to also thank my senior colleague, Professor P. K. Misra, for going through the handwritten version of this manuscript and making many valuable suggestions. I am particularly thankful to Professor Lionel Caplan, Professor A. K. Danda and Dr. Andrew Russell for their valuable suggestions on an earlier draft. I must not forget here the help of my brother-in-law, Wing Commander N. K. Taneja, and his wife Roshan.

I now thank my parents, my wife Roshina, and our daughter Tarona, for ungrudgingly facing the hard times, with or without me, and making this effort a success.

1

Introduction

The Problem

In the geographically contiguous areas of Darjeeling, Sikkim and Nepal there has recently been a mushrooming of organisations which seek to preserve and develop their indigenous culture, language and religion. More than a dozen such groups in Nepal have established their branches wherever their members live. Another half dozen have emerged in Sikkim. However, in Darjeeling, some of these associations date back to the beginning of this century while a few are fairly recent. Darjeeling became a part of India in the mid-nineteenth century and its relative political openness allowed such organisations to come up quite early. In contrast, the hereditary and theocratic rule in Sikkim and Nepal have opened up only very recently.

Despite an earlier emergence, most of Darjeeling's indigenous organisations have had little impact on the cultural and political history of the region. The living conditions in Darjeeling after it came under Bengal in 1866 were not conducive to their growth. The political and cultural pressures of a numerically dominant and educationally far 'superior' Bengali 'race' (see Smith 1993 for the concept) forced the various communities like the Gurung, Tamang, Mangar, Rai and Limbu to come under the umbrella of the Nepali or Gorkhali nation (nation meaning peoples here, not nation-state). Their respective identities had to be submerged in order to constitute a force strong enough to resist Bengali domination and ensure their common survival. Thus, they became a part of the Gorkhali or Nepali people and the Nepali language became their language as well. In the process, their own languages and scripts were pushed into oblivion, often unable to be revived due to inadequate numbers of speakers in a particular locality.

If such were the reasons for the various communities like the Limbu, Newar, Rai and Gurung to be deprived of their culture, language and religion in Darjeeling, the conditions in Sikkim were similar to those existing in Nepal. The Buddhist theocratic and hereditary rulers there did not allow such groups to come together nor did they recognise the cultural, linguistic and religious heterogeneity within the so-called Nepalis. To them, such communities were basically 'migrants' from Nepal, Hindus by religion and 'troublesome as neighbours'.

This perception of the Bhutia rulers in Sikkim was primarily shaped by their long historical interaction with the Gorkhas. Such interactions were characterised by internecine wars which forced the Bhutias to gradually shift their capital from the west to the east of the kingdom. With little social involvement with the Nepalis even after 1890, which marked the end of the Gorkha–Sikkim wars, they remained oblivious of the cultural and other kinds of heterogeneity within the Nepalis. This happened due to ecological as well as political reasons. The Bhutias lived in the higher elevations and were concentrated in the present northern district of Sikkim, entry into which was politically forbidden to the Nepalis. However, they made one exception in this regard—to recognise the Limbus or Chongs as a separate community from the rest of the Nepalis and extend some privileges to them.

In Nepal, the Gorkha rulers were acutely aware of the cultural, linguistic and other differences across communities but they were not officially recognised as separate nationalities. They were essentially treated as subjugated or conquered peoples who needed to be brought under the Nepali nation. Prithivinarayan Shah, the Gorkha king who was responsible for politically demarcating the present boundaries of Nepal in the early 1770s, had metaphorically set the official attitude towards such people when he described Nepal as 'a garden of four varnas and thirty-six jats'. The different peoples were, in other words, just different flowers in a garden, or 'castes' which are organically related to each other. This analogy has great symbolic value for the ruling elite and most mainstream scholars in Nepal even today represent the official attitude towards the various nationalities there.

The situation, however, changed when Sikkim became a part of India in 1975, Darjeeling suspended the Gorkhaland Movement and settled for the Darjeeling Gorkha Hill Council in 1988, and Nepal yielded to democratic forces in 1990. While the background of the national leaders in Nepal is still largely the same, Sikkim was briefly ruled by a Bhutia Chief Minister (Kazi Lhendup Dorjee Khangsarpa) before it came under the rule of a Chhetri Chief Minister (Nar Bahadur Bhandari) in 1979 and remained so for about fifteen years. Darjeeling has a Tamang (Subhas Ghisingh) holding the post of the chairman of the Darjeeling Gorkha Hill Council. The Bhandari rule in Sikkim was, however, possible not only due to Nar Bahadur Bhandari's charisma, as some argue, but also to the synthesised Nepali nationalism developed there over a long period of time by the Bhutia rulers.

The United Nations declaration of 1993 as the Year of the Indigenous Peoples gave further impetus to the already changed political climate and brought a new lease of life to the marginalised and subjugated communities in the region. They began to organise themselves vigorously in search of lost identities.

The present situation is characterised by an active process of reinventing linkages not only within such classified groups like Limbu, Rai and Tamang but also at the level of cognate concepts like 'Kirata', 'Janajati' and 'Mongol'. The profile of various such organisations provided in Chapter 8 indicates that they are trying to recreate their culture, religion and language primarily at the former level. While the Tagadhari category representing the Bahun, Thakuri and Chhetri castes constitutes an objective entity, the essentialised Kirata, Janajati or Mongol identity is yet to evolve fully as its anti-thesis. The people designated as 'Kiratas' here are yet to crystallise their ideology and culture. They still seem to vacillate between the relatively single and simple delineations such as the Limbu or Khambu and the more compound and complex characterisations like Kirata, Janajati or Mongol.

Due to the changed situation, the historically marginalised communities are now seeking to challenge the hegemony of the Tagadharis (high castes like the Bahun, Thakuri and Chhetri) and are in the process of 'inventing' their national consciousness. There has begun, to borrow from Foucault, an 'insurrection of subjugated knowledges'. The 'subjugated knowledges', according to him, refer to "a whole set of knowledges that have been disqualified as inadequate to their task or insufficiently elaborated: naive knowledges, located low down on the hierarchy, beneath the required level of cognition or scientificity" (1980:82). This would not be possible without the changed political climate of the region. But it is desirable to understand why there is a sudden need to 'imagine' these nationalities.

Politics of Culture

The concept of 'culture' not only varies according to the aspects emphasised by various anthropologists but also according to the time it has passed through. There are endless—some already dated—debates over whether it is value-free or value-loaded, society-specific or universal, hierarchical or differential, process or structure, material or non-material, and so on. One also notices a shift in its focus on material artefacts to the more abstract, formal and conceptual aspects in the post 1950s (see Bauman 1973). Recent conceptualisations of culture, for instance, speak of it as a system of meanings, ideologies, unconscious structures.

Towards further elaboration of this concept, Laitin (1977) draws attention to the hegemonic nature of culture. According to him the "[p]olitical elites in any society will act strategically and ideologically in the hope of defining and delimiting which strands of their society's culture should become dominant. Those who are successful in establishing a dominant cultural framework form a 'hegemonic bloc'" (1977:171). But since hegemony can only create a dominant subsystem and cannot "create a congruent and harmonious social system", he concludes that the "non-marginal affronts to the commonsensical order are inherent in all hegemonic structures" (1977:183).

Another aspect of culture that may be brought to bear on the discussion here is its use in what is called 'reconstructive ethnography'. Such an ethnography overlooks the social and historical conditioning of culture because it presupposes that the indigenous cultures succumb under the impact of 'civilisation' and exist as a category of 'traditional remains'. Such cultures are not only assumed to be 'static' but the people representing them are even branded as people without a culture (Devalle 1992:40).

Culture may perhaps be seen here as a symbolic system within which a group of people operate in order to perpetuate or fight against a 'hegemony' which is defined as "the political forging—whether through coercion or elite bargaining—and institutionalization of a pattern of group activity in a state and the concurrent idealization of that schema into a dominant symbolic framework that reigns as common sense" (Laitin 1977:183). In other words, culture is not an independent or isolated symbol in harmonious equilibrium with another culture but it is a system in constant conflict within and with other cultures for better appropriation of the available resources of a state. This should not, however, be construed to mean that there was no culture prior to the emergence of the state. It was there, in hierarchical relationship with other cultures, but it was then governed by traditions. The hierarchy assumed the relationships of superordination and subordination after the emergence of the state.

Another concept which is politically akin to the concept of culture is 'nationalism' which, according to Gellner, is "primarily a political principle, which holds that the political and the national unit should be congruent" (1987:1). P. H. van der Plank makes it more explicit when he defines it as "an ideology consisting of values, symbols, norms and expectations, living in a social collectivity (group) and based on belief in a common descent and, as a consequence, a common destiny, strong enough to desire to maintain, strengthen or create a formally and legally organized society" (1975:9).

One of the problems with this concept is that such an 'ideology' may be confined to a nation or, more frequently, extended to a nation-state (Kohn 1968:63). When it is used in the former sense it is often qualified as 'ethno-nationalism', 'proto-nationalism', 'sub-nationalism', 'fissiparous-nationalism', 'mini-nationalism', and what have you.

Nationalism, as it is understood by Louis L. Snyder, is: "A condition of mind, feeling, or sentiment of a group of people living in a well-defined geographic area, speaking a common language, possessing a literature in which their aspirations are expressed, attached to common traditions and customs, venerating their own heroes, and, in some cases, having the same religion" (1982:xv). The problem here is that there are many nations like the Jewish and the Palestinian which cannot be fitted into this.

The boundaries of a culture or nation and a nation-state seldom overlap but both involve a similar process of nation-building. This process invariably involves homogenisation of cultural and ideological values within a group or a number of groups, which means imposition of the ideology, norms and values of the hegemonic group on the marginal groups. While the Limbus (or the Rais) resist cultural or linguistic standardisation by the Tagadharis, they also carry out the same process within their own groups. What is resisted at the level of the nation-state is thus perpetrated at the level of a culture or nation.

The appeal of culture in all such nation-building processes is unquestionable. Spencer has illustrated this well with his study of Sinhala culture and nationalism (1990). Gellner has gone even further to define 'nation' in terms of culture though he is equally aware of the 'voluntaristic' aspect of the concept of nation. According to him, "Two men are of the same nation if and only if they share the same culture, where culture in turn means a system of ideas and signs and associations and ways of behaving and communicating" (1987:7).

The relationship between culture and nationalism has assumed renewed significance after the emergence of the concept of 'national culture'. Its relationship with the nationalist ideology is, according to Richard Fox, "contingent and processual: the creation of nationalist ideologies anticipates a larger project, the forming or reforming of a national culture" (1990:4). He further writes: "A national culture starts out as a nationalist ideology, that is, a consciousness or perception of what the nation is or should be, which then may gain public meaning and be put into action. Usually there are several co-existing and even contradictory perceptions, which constitute competitive nationalist ideologies" (1990:4).

It is here that Benedict Anderson's phrase 'imagined community' (1991) becomes contextual. Like national culture, the imagined community is not given but consciously created. The word 'imagined' may be, perhaps justifiably, equated with Hobsbawm's 'invention' and defined operationally as a 'construction'. In this sense, a nation is 'imagined' because, as Anderson writes, "the members of even the smallest nation will never know most of their fellow-members, meet them, or even hear of them, yet in the minds of each lives the image of their communion" (1991:6). He goes on to explain the nationalist upsurges in modern times as functions of "cultural roots" rather than "self-consciously-held political ideologies" (1991:12). The importance of culture in relation to nationalism has also been recently illustrated with the case of the Oromo speakers in Africa (see Baxter 1993).

However, the link between culture and nationalism has assumed added significance particularly because the state has grown conceptually incompatible with culture (Nandy 1997) and it has virtually turned out to be the patron of the dominant culture. It is such a failure of the state that has been primarily responsible for the subjugated cultures redefining their cultural and national boundaries.

The present study is an attempt to establish the relationship between the state or the surrogate community and the politics of marginalised cultures or nations on the basis of historical as well as ethnographic data on three Kirata communities living in the eastern Himalayas—the Limbu, Khambu or Rai, and the Yakkha.

The Fieldwork and the Field

Fieldwork is considered indispensable in any anthropological study that deals with contemporary society. The early fieldwork tradition established by anthropologists like Malinowski and Radcliffe-Brown is still taken as the ideal, particularly in terms of the length of stay and acquisition of the native languages. Many European and American universities are trying to live up to this ideal even today. But much has changed in this tradition after the 1950s, particularly in studies of the post-colonial world. This anthropology operates mostly within a familiar universe though the exact language/dialect and place may not have been known before. The norms and values are not as different as they were between the European anthropologists and their Orients.

In India, post-colonial anthropology cannot be considered to be different from the colonial. The old boundaries between Subject and Object are redrawn within the country. Only certain categories of people such as the tribals, minorities or frontier peoples are taken as Objects and certain others take on the role of Subjects (though they themselves may have been Objects for the European or American anthropologists). The language and mind-set of the Subjects in terms of ethnographic representation are much the same as in colonial anthropology (Po'dar and Subba, 1991).

Where do I place my study of the Kiratas in such a tradition? I belong to one of the Kirata communities dealt with here – the Limbu – and have a distant Yakkha matrilineage as well. I was trained in an ethnographic tradition which was largely colonial but I have felt a strong sense of dissatisfaction with it. I feel dishonest when I write 'they' when I refer to my own community. I have lived and grown up with many of them. Will my research be branded as 'unscientific' or 'biased' if I write 'we'? Do I have to refer to my own people as 'they'? I do not seem to have much of a choice.

The selection of field sites for this study was governed by my 'subconscious mind', shaped by my conviction that the villages should be representative. But I could not afford to study more than three villages, one each for the three Kirata communities. My teaching and administrative responsibilities would not allow time for fieldwork outside of vacations and semester breaks.

I discussed the objectives of my study and the villages where I could possibly conduct my fieldwork with knowledgeable persons in Kathmandu and Kalimpong. I soon had an exhaustive list of the districts and villages. Deciding on the Sankhuwa Sabha and Bhojpur districts to study the Yakkhas and Rais respectively was rather easy as only one or two persons had suggested otherwise. But in the case of the Limbus, the Panchthar district was decided upon after due deliberation over the merits of the Terethum district in east Nepal and the West district of Sikkim, each promising to be more representative of the Limbu culture and society than the other. But, since I had already done my doctoral research in Sikkim, I decided to work in Nepal for this study. Between May 1992 and January 1993, I undertook reconnaissance visits to the three districts chosen and finally settled on Yangnam village in Panchthar district, Madi Mulkharka in Sankhuwa Sabha district, and Chhinamakhu in Bhojpur district as the best possible sites for my fieldwork.

During this period, I spent some time in Kathmandu, working in various libraries and interviewing scholars and Kirata leaders. I also went to Darjeeling and Sikkim to do similar work. A village in east Nepal often extends over a whole mountain and walking from one end to the other, vertically or horizontally, may take about half a day or more. In terms of geographical area it may extend between fifty and a hundred square kilometres and comprise about 800 to 1200 households. Each ward is often as big as a whole village in Darjeeling and Sikkim. Even the altitude range of a village in east Nepal is at least 1000 metres whereas it is only about 300 metres in Darjeeling and Sikkim. Despite the vastness and an apparent lack of compactness, villagers in Nepal can count and identify almost every household in their village. Almost every educated male head of a household is able to map out clans and lineages in the entire village.

For these reasons, the strategy of fieldwork in east Nepal villages had to be different from that in Darjeeling and Sikkim. Merely taking the census of household members, livestock and land for about a thousand households, spread over at least fifty square kilometres, and with an altitude range of about 1000 metres would have taken at least six months. Time was at a premium and I had, therefore, to be content with scaling down the work. I made a list of the various social groups in each village and simultaneously collected information on the approximate number of households as well as their distribution. On the basis of this list, I made a stratified random sampling of about ten per cent of the households which I visited and collected census data as well as information on their culture and nationalism.

The Field Sites

Yangnam: The village of Yangnam is located in the Panchthar district of east Nepal. The nearest urban centre is Fidim, the headquarters of this district, which is about twenty kilometres away. It is about a six to eight hours' walk from Fidim to Yangnam though many young men of the village can reportedly reach Fidim and return to Yangnam on the same day. Hiley is another town where the villagers of the northern fringe buy their necessities but this town is inaccessible during the rainy season due to landslides and flooding rivers.

Yangnam is bounded on the north by the Hewa khola (*khola*=river), on the east by the Papungden khola, and on the south and west by the Khong khola. Thus, it is surrounded by rivers which are almost totally dry in winter but difficult to cross in summer. There is a concrete bridge constructed recently over the Hewa and there are temporary bridges of logs and bamboo over other streams. The village is divided horizontally by an arterial road which is about five feet wide whereas other village roads are rather narrow and not well maintained.

The altitude of this village ranges approximately from 610 metres at Hewa khola to about 2200 metres at Akashe hamlet. Beyond this altitude extend uninhabited areas which are used only for grazing in summer. The temperature varies from 0 to about 27 degrees centrigrade and the village receives adequate rainfall. Except for some hamlets in the eastern part, the village receives adequate sunshine too.

There is one Madhyamik Vidyalaya (upto Class X), nine primary schools, two temples, a health post, an agriculture centre, a veterinary centre, the village post office, the Gaon Vikas Samiti building and the cooperative office. Khalangatar hamlet, where most of these are concentrated, looks like a semi-urban settlement. It also has general stores and tailoring shops. The ruins of an ancient fort, which was once a royal outpost, is also visible near the Madhyamik Vidyalaya.

The number of households in the village is not known exactly. My own estimate of the total is 873, of which I covered 112 households. Table I shows the distribution of households over the various Limbu clans and other castes/communities in the village.

Table I: ***Limbu clans and other castes/communities in Yangnam***

Limbu clans & other castes/communities	*Estimated No. of households*	*No. of actually covered households*
Angbo	2	1
Ekten	15	3
Hangsurumba	77	8
Jabegou	321	32
Kerung	142	14
Khajum	19	3
Kurungbang	3	1
Lawati	2	1
Lowa	23	4
Manglak	2	1
Mangmu	24	4

Limbu clans & other castes/communities	*Estimated No. of households*	*No. of actually covered households*
Nembeku	2	1
Nembhang	10	2
Phago	17	3
Songpangphe	2	1
Suhang	1	1
Tamling	7	1
Thamsuhang	94	11
Thebe	1	1
Yokwa	1	1
Younghang	1	1
Bahun	32	3
Chhetri	14	2
Damai	11	3
Kami	23	3
Newar	1	1
Rai	14	3
Sarki	12	2
Total	873	112

Source: Fieldwork, 1992–93

During the fieldwork I observed that the clans/castes/communities with the larger number of households are the earlier settlers of the village. Table II shows their distribution over various hamlets and wards.

Table II: ***Distribution of Limbu clans and other castes/communities in Yangnam***

Ward No.	*Tols/Hamlets*	*Limbu clans & other castes/communities*
1	Aasmane, Pachise, Chilingden	Lowa, Hangsurumba, Lawati, Jabegou, Thamsuhang, Sarki, Bahun, Rai
2	Thangnapa	Jabegou, Thamsuhang, Bahun
3	Damsidabba, Phasingla	Jabegou, Nembhang, Nembeku, Angbo, Damai
4	Etembe, Lungchokthoba	Jabegou, Thamsuhang
5	Magarcheppa, Khalangatar, Sapnuwa, Padamdhoka	Jabegou, Kerung, Hangsurumba, Ekten, Khajum, Kami
6	Gahirigaon, Kakchuwa	Jabegou, Kerung, Hangsurumba, Ekten, Damai
7	Akashe, Surkenangi	Jabegou, Ekten, Khajum, Songpangphe, Kurungbang, Thamsuhang
8	Angepa, Bansbote, Hamrang	Jabegou, Lowa, Kerung, Tamling, Rai, Mangmu, Bahun
9	Luwafu, Tercheni	Kerung, Mangmu, Tamling, Jabegou, Bahun

Source: Fieldwork, 1992

Table II shows that some larger groups are distributed over more than one hamlet and ward. In other words, there is no clear concentration of any clan/caste/community in any ward. In view of this distribution, the argument of some respondents that the village was originally inhabited by the Thegim clan seems plausible. This clan had four lineages, viz., Chabegou (later adapted as Jabegou), Kerung, Hangsurumba and Thaklehang, of which the last seems to have been replaced by the term Thamsuhang. It is quite probable that other Limbu clans and non-Limbu castes/communities joined them later and contributed to the heterogeneity of each hamlet found today.

Table III: ***Social categories and population in Yangnam***

Social categories	*Male*	*Female*	*Total*	*%*
Tagadhari	17	14	31	4.3
Kirata	305	326	631	87.3
Other	3	3	6	0.8
Untouchable	32	23	55	7.6
Total	357	366	723	100.0

Source: Fieldwork, 1992

In Table III the people of the village have been classified under four social categories and this classification has been followed throughout this book. The Tagadhari category includes the Bahun, Thakuri and Chhetri; the Kiratas include the Limbu, Rai and Yakkha; Other Mongoloids include communities some of which are considered as Kiratas by a few people but are not included under the 'Kirata' category in this book; and finally, the Untouchable castes—Kami, Sarki and Damai or Darji.

Srikhalangatar Madhyamik Vidyalaya, the only secondary school in the village, was established as a primary school in 1971 and upgraded in 1979. There are about 450 students and 18 teachers. Of the 18 teachers, nine are Bahun, eight Limbu and one Yadav from the terai of Nepal. This school also serves as the venue for the Gaon Vikas Samiti meetings and polling centres.

The houses in the village are remarkably similar. The walls are made of stone and mud and daubed with red mud or ochre. The architecture is also monotonously similar: houses are diagonal and normally consist of three storeys; the lowest storey being used for cooking, storing water and receiving guests or visitors; the middle for sleeping and storing food grains, malts or liquor; and the uppermost floor for household or clan deities. There are small wooden windows and doors but no ventilation for smoke to escape except through the square apertures between the storeys created by the wooden beams. Though it affects the lungs and eyes of the inhabitants, the smoke is valued for its ability to protect the timber and bamboo from insects and to preserve meat and food grains.

The houses are generally solidly built. The windows and doors are fitted without nails or hinges. The roof is normally thatched with wild grass of different varieties, or with locally made terracotta tiles. Only a few rich families have their roofs covered with corrugated or galvanized iron sheets. Every house has a front verandah where visitors are received and bamboo baskets are woven when it is hot or raining outside.

The denuding of neighbourhood forests has led to an increasing scarcity of firewood and fodder for cattle. And the people need firewood in plenty in order to cook, prepare malt or liquor, cook fodder for their cattle and to keep themselves warm. Many spring water sources have also dried up. Though the government has now made provisions for supplying water through iron pipes in many villages, such water is often available only for a couple of hours a day.

Chhinamakhu: Chhinamakhu is situated in the Bhojpur district of Nepal. The nearest urban centre is Bhojpur town, which is also the administrative headquarters of this district. The village is roughly 20 kilometres to the northeast of this town and it takes about eight hours on foot to get there. The road passes through a number of villages and rivers. Chhinamakhu is bounded on the east by Timma village, on the west by Annapurna, on the north by dense forested hills including the Merong peak, and on the south by the Yangtang and Pikhuwa rivers. There is a suspension bridge over the Pikhuwa which makes it possible for the villagers of Annapurna and Chhinamakhu to go to Bhojpur even during the rainy season. Innumerable small streams flow down the hills and can be crossed easily on small bamboo bridges.

The altitude of this village and other geographical features are similar to those of Yangnam, but the land is generally more fertile and a number of perennial streams have made irrigation possible over a much larger area. The dense forest at the top of the village serves as the catchment area for the rivers and as a pasture for cattle during the summer. In winter, the forest area is usually covered with snow. Chhinamakhu also receives better sunshine than Yangnam.

Apart from its well-carved terraces and sweet oranges, Chhinamakhu is famous in the district for the leaders it has produced. Dhyan Bahadur Rai, once a minister and now a Raj Sabha (Upper House of the Parliament of Nepal) member; Sangram Rai, once the president of the Bhojpur

District Development Council; and Shashi Bhushan Kirant, the present incumbent of this office, are all from this village. It has also produced doctors, engineers, and accomplished musicians like Bulu Mukarung. Foreign scholars like Simon Sinclair from England, Richard English of the New School for Social Research, New York, and the noted linguist Boyd Michailovsky have all stayed here at various times.

Like in Yangnam, there is only one Madhyamik school though there are primary schools in each ward. The hamlet Devithan closely resembles Khalangatar of Yangnam, with the temple, post office, shops, health centre, agriculture and veterinary office, and most importantly, the Sri Tribhuwan Dharmodaya Madhyamik Vidyalaya located within it. Like Khalangatar again, this hamlet is the cultural, business and political centre of the village.

Some data on Rai clans and other castes/communities are presented in Table IV.

Table IV: ***Rai clans and other castes/communities in Chhinamakhu***

Rai clans & other castes/communities	*Estimated No. of households*	*No. of actually covered households*
Chamling	3	1
Charghare	22	2
Dilpali	13	2
Dumi	2	1
Huongchen	13	2
Ishara	2	1
Khamtu	40	4
Khamyoungkha	7	1
Kulunge	22	3
Kwoyu	300	25
Pewang	1	1
Rupabung	6	1
Sangpang	2	1
Siptungkha	200	19
Thulunge	9	2
Bahun	2	1
Chhetri	60	6
Damai	14	2
Gurung	22	2
Kami	15	2
Sherpa	12	1
Tamang	4	1
Total	771	81

Source: Fieldwork, 1993

The number of Kwoyu households being higher than that of the Siptungkhas theoretically suggests that the former are earlier settlers than the latter. But even the Kwoyus admit that they are later settlers than the Siptungkhas, who were the first to settle in this village after driving away a group called the Chongdongs.

Table V: ***Distribution of Rai clans and other castes/communities in Chhinamakhu***

Ward No.	Tols/Hamlets	Rai clans & other castes/communities
1	Choudhe, Ekhang, Khebang, Ambote, Sheerdalee, Chamlakha, Kokachong, Thalakham, Suntale	Huongchen, Siptungkha, Charghare Kwoyu, Thulunge, Khamtu, Chhetri Sangpang, Ishara, Chamling, Dumi
2	Devithan, Begtuwa, Banstola, Kwoyutola, Sakewatol	Khamyongkha, Charghare, Kwoyu, Dilpali, Khamtu
3	Tentola, Bakhim, Neware Danra, Maksahut	Huongchen, Siptungkha, Charghare, Kwoyu, Thulunge, Khamtu, Kami, Damai
4	Munbala, Churbuk, Tamlakha	Kwoyu, Kulunge, Khamtu, Tamang
5	Naulagaon, Ghorenangi	Kami, Gurung, Sherpa, Chhetri, Bahun
6	Dhunge, Chukhalung, Dorosa, Bhirkuna	Siptungkha, Dilpali, Khamtu
7	Yangchentar	Kami, Tamang, Chhetri
8	Rumla, Panche, Kangkang	Kami, Gurung, Sherpa, Chhetri
9	Khaila, Wadungla, Bobob, Luknagi	Khamyongkha, Gurung, Chhetri

Source: Fieldwork, 1993

Table V shows that the numerically important clan/caste/community is distributed over more than one *tol* or ward and there is no *tol* which is homogenous in composition. However, most of the hamlets are numerically dominated by a single or two clans/castes/communities. The heterogeneity continues to grow with migrants trickling in mainly from the west.

Table VI: ***Social categories and population in Chhinamakhu***

Social categories	*Male*	*Female*	*Total*	*%*
Tagadhari	52	56	108	23.5
Kirata	146	133	279	60.6
Other Mongoloid	35	26	61	13.3
Untouchable	7	5	12	2.6
Total	240	220	460	100.0

Source: Fieldwork, 1993

The percentage of the Kirata population in this village is much lower (60.6) than in Yangnam (87.3). On the other hand, the Tagadharis and

Other Mongoloids have a much higher percentage (23.5 and 13.3 respectively) compared to Yangnam (4.3 and 0.8 respectively). The higher percentage of the non-Kiratas in this village is perhaps partly due to its location, which is more accessible to people of other origins migrating from the west.

The architecture, painting and other details of the houses in Chhinamakhu are almost the same as those observed in Yangnam. The only difference, though rather important culturally, between a Limbu and a Rai house is that the latter has a separate room for the household deity. This room is normally located on the top floor though it may also be located on the middle floor. The Rai houses also have separate hearths made of three stones erected vertically and non-Kiratas are not allowed to go or sit near them.

Another interesting feature of this village which is conspicuous by its absence in Yangnam and elsewhere in Panchthar is the memorial stone slabs prominently erected on road sides, specially at resting places. Such slabs contain carvings of the sun, half-moon, bow and arrow, the trident of Lord Shiva and the name and dates of birth and death of the deceased person. This is not only interesting as a register of the indigenous population, but it also indicates that the art of writing or carving has existed among them from earlier times. The names and other details being written in the Devanagari script also shows that this script has found better acceptance than with the Limbus who are proud of their own script, although most of them can neither read nor write it.

Further evidence of the Rais being more Nepalicised is found in their day-to-day conversation which is rarely in their own language. This is not so in Yangnam. The Limbus not only have a better command over their language but also use it more commonly than do the Rais, who often use their language only to communicate some secret information in the presence of non-Rai strangers.

Madi Mulkharka: Madi Mulkharka is in the Sankhuwa Sabha district which was historically within the territory of Limbuan. Basantpur town is about a six hour walk and Tumlingtar which has an aerodrome and which is situated on the bank of the Sabha river is almost equally distant. But since the former town is much larger and the shopping cheaper, the villagers prefer to go there rather than to Tumlingtar. A weekly market is held at Madi Rambeni village and most people go there to collect their daily necessities.

Madi Mulkharka is bounded on the east by Terethum district, on the west by Madi Rambeni village, on the north by Mawdin village, and on the south by the Maya khola and Tamaphok village across this river. The road from Madi Rambeni to Terethum divides the village horizontally into two equal halves. There are many streams flowing down to Maya khola and there are innumerable bamboo bridges over those streams most of which dry up in winter. Each of these bridges is maintained by a rich household nearby.

The altitude range and temperature variation in the village are almost the same as in the other two villages. A greater part of the village faces east, and so there is plenty of sunlight. But compared to the other two villages, the extent of cultivable land is less. However, cardamom cultivation in the wastelands along the streams is more extensive in this village. There is little forest cover in the pasture lands at the top of the village and scarcity of firewood is more acute here. The cardamom fields have several trees but they are not cut.

Madi Mulkharka is famous for its extensive cardamom cultivation. An annual fete of three days is held in this village at the end of January when people from all surrounding villages and districts gather to gamble and merry-make. There is also a huge playground donated by one Man Bahadur Majiya, where inter-village volleyball and football tournaments are held during the fete. Some of the people of this village have also risen to the status of ministers, college teachers and important leaders of the district.

Like in Yangnam and Chhinamakhu, there is one prominent hamlet called Mulkharka which has the semblance of a small township. Though primary schools are established in every ward, only this hamlet has a secondary school. It also has shops, a health centre, an agriculture and a veterinary office, a Gaon Vikas Samiti office, a post office and the Nepal Red Cross Society office, besides a mill run on hydro-electricity for grinding rice, wheat, millets and mustard seeds. The demand for this mill is so great that its owner has recently acquired another run on diesel.

Table VII depicts the number of households in 1987 belonging to Yakkhas and other castes/communities.

Table VII: ***Yakkhas and other castes/communities in Madi Mulkharka***

Yakkhas & other castes/communities	*Total No. of households (1987)*	*No. of actually covered households*
Bahun	118	9
Chhetri	578	41
Damai	48	3
Gharti/Bhujel	12	2
Gurung	187	13
Jimi (Yakkha)	234	17

Yakkhas & other castes/communities	*Total No. of households (1987)*	*No. of actually covered households*
Kami	62	5
Limbu	9	2
Newar	47	3
Sarki	11	1
Sherpa	118	3
Tamang	46	4
Total	1470	103

Source: Gaon Vikas Samiti Office, Madi Mulkharka, 1993

It is clear that the Kiratas in the village do not constitute more than 16.5% of the total number of households in the village. Here it should be pointed out that the actual numerical status of the Jimis or Yakkhas as 234 households is misleading because even ethnic Rais have been reportedly mistaken for Yakkhas. For instance, the Nechali, Amchoke and Mangpang Rais of Thulo Wairang (Ward No. 8) have been counted along with other Yakkhas but these are ethnic Rai clans. This confusion is because of the absence of widespread ethnic consciousness among the Yakkhas living there. One may also interpret this phenomenon as a case of the existence of fluid ethnic boundaries between them and the native Rais as a consequence of the granting of various titles (like 'Rai') since the 1770s in Nepal. Other reasons that may be attributed to this phenomenon are the Yakkhas' small numerical size and intermarriages with the Rais and Limbus of the surrounding areas. The fictive kinship network that has developed over the years between them and other social groups, particularly the Bahun, Chhetri and the Gurung is also a factor in this regard.

Table VIII: ***Distribution of Yakkha and other castes/communities in Madi Mulkharka***

Ward No.	*Tols/Hamlets*	*Yakkhas & other castes/communities*
1	Hulaki Gaon, Srijung, Toribari, Pindalu Danra	Bahun, Limbu, Bhujel, Kami, Sarki. Damai
2	Ghimire Gaon, Dabale, Soti	Bahun, Chhetri, Newar, Sherpa, Bhujel, Kami
3	Chowki, Kattike Gufa, Ale Danra, Danratol, Madamsingh, Solaban	Chhetri, Tamang Bahun, Kami
4	Waling, Jimi Gaon	Yakkha, Damai
5	Madi, Singhare Bhir, Tham Kharka, Siddhanagi	Yakkha, Gurung, Sherpa
6	Majh Kharka, Hanglafu, Mulkharka	Yakkha, Gurung, Bahun, Newar, Kami
7	Ahale, Mele, Phudung	Gurung, Chhetri, Yakkha

Ward No.	Tols/Hamlets	Yakkhas & other castes/communities
8	Kanpur, Wairang, Gahiri Gaon, Aiselu	Yakkha, Chhetri, Rai, Limbu, Newar, Gurung
9	Umling, Echcharam	Yakkha, Chhetri, Rai, Damai

Source: Fieldwork, 1993

In the table above, a few hamlets like Ghimire Gaon and Jimi Gaon have been named after a sub-caste or community but in fact no hamlet is entirely inhabited by any particular caste or community though each is numerically dominated by a particular Yakkha clan, caste, or community.

Table IX: ***Social categories and population in Madi Mulkharka***

Social categories	*Male*	*Female*	*Total*	*%*
Tagadhari	108	92	200	42.4
Kirata	35	43	78	16.5
Other Mongoloid	69	74	143	30.3
Untouchable	27	24	51	10.8
Total	239	233	472	100.0

Source: Fieldwork, 1993

Table IX clearly shows the numerical insignificance of the Kiratas whose percentage is only slightly higher than that of the Untouchables. However, due to certain historical and other reasons, it is still the Yakkhas who call the shots there, so to speak, and only recently are the Chhetris and Gurungs trying to challenge the political hegemony of the Yakkhas in the village.

The relative absence of the memorial stone slabs is striking after crossing the Sabha river which separates Limbuan from Khambuan. This is another indication of the fact that the Yakkhas are culturally closer to the Limbus than the Rais. Otherwise. the architecture, raw materials and other details of the houses are, internally as well as externally, quite the same as observed in the other two villages. However, the use of corrugated and galvanized iron sheets for roofing is more common here which is probably due to the relative closeness to Basantpur and the economic surplus generated by cardamom cultivation in this village.

Forty-five per cent of the Yakkha respondents claimed that they could speak their language though in practice they seldom did so. Their condition is, in fact, worse than that of the Rais some of whom can speak their language at least within the family. Thus their Nepalicisation seems to be greater than that of the Rais of Chhinamakhu. This may perhaps be, as already discussed, attributed to their insignificant demographic size and the lack of ethnic consciousness among them.

The description of Yangnam, Chhinamakhu and Madi Mulkharka villages reveals many similarities among them which are briefly summarised here. First, the altitude range, temperature variation and other environmental conditions are similar in the three villages. Even the vegetation, animals reared and crops grown are the same.

Second, the raw materials, architecture and other details of their houses are also similar. Besides, the way their houses are daubed or painted are the same. The internal arrangement of the Rai houses is slightly different from the arrangement of Limbu and Yakkha houses but there is little external difference across the three villages.

Third, the settlement pattern, which is highly heterogeneous down to the *tol* level, is also similar in the three villages studied. Each *tol* may be dominated by a particular clan, caste or community but no *tol* is completely homogenous in composition. The settlement pattern is uniformly scattered except in one hamlet in each village where some clustering of the houses can be seen.

Fourth, the original inhabitants are gradually turning into a minority due primarily to migration of people from outside. Despite the three villages being more or less equidistant from the nearest urban centre, the Yakkhas already seem to have turned into an insignificant minority in their village. If this is taken as an indication of the demographic change in east Nepal, the same fate may befall the Rais and Limbus after some decades.

Fifth, proficiency in their native language seems to be declining gradually in the whole of east Nepal and the influence of the Nepali language is becoming all pervasive. While the Limbus are still successful to some extent in retaining their language they have already become bilingual. Even with the strong sense of their identity, the future of their language perhaps depends more on the state apparatus than their own ethnic organisations.

Sixth, natural resources like water, fodder and firewood are gradually shrinking due to population increase and continued land reclamation for various uses. If this continues unabated, a time may soon come when the social matrix may have to be changed in order to ensure survival in a competitive situation. The relationship between the 'original inhabitants' and 'later migrants' may change and create new ethnic boundaries as witnessed in many parts of the eastern Himalayas.

Finally, a word about rampant alcoholism. While the cultural milieu is congenial to imbibing alcohol, excessive indulgence is not always appreciated by the people. There are several excessive drinkers in every village especially among the non-Tagadhari categories, thereby justifying the appellation 'matwali' for them. Worse still, there are some in every village who are addicted to taking harmful drugs, which is a habit they attribute to their stay in the northeastern parts of India. Smoking cheap cigarettes or bidis is common among both men and women, adults as well as adolescents. The situation is now so deplorable that no one will undertake paid work in the fields unless some kind of alcohol is offered to him or her. Even the Tagadharis are sometimes compelled to offer alcohol to their non-Tagadhari workers though there is a strong cultural inhibition among them to do so.

Darjeeling and Sikkim

No intensive fieldwork was proposed to be conducted in Darjeeling and Sikkim for the purpose of the present study. However, for the benefit of those who are not acquainted with this region, the description of a few salient features may be in order (for details, see Subba 1985b, 1989).

The Kirata communities cannot claim to be wholly native to this region. Written history shows that the ancestors of many Kirata people living here have come from Nepal. The only community which is known to have originally inhabited this region is the Lepcha. Though, notionally, most of the land here once belonged to this community, over the last 150 years or so this community, like the Kiratas in east Nepal, has been reduced to an insignificant minority.

The villages in Darjeeling and Sikkim are socially much more complex. Each village represents many more castes, communities and religions than do the villages in east Nepal. Though much smaller in geographical area, the villages here are in every respect more plural in composition as well as character. There is hardly any linguistic community which has a number sizeable enough to sustain its own language. As a result, 'Nepali' is not only the lingua franca but the mother-tongue of almost all the inhabitants. Knowledge of one's own language is definitely very poor, even non-existent. Thus 'Nepali' assumes a distinct identity of a community in the Indian diaspora whereas in Nepal, it only refers to their nationality or *rastriyata*. The peoples living in Nepal belong to specific communities like Newar, Rai, Limbu, Mangar and Gurung but never to a 'Nepali' community. It is for this reason that each community has retained the knowledge of its language, customs and traditions to a great extent in Nepal. It is only recently that the various communities in

Darjeeling and Sikkim have become aware of the need for a revival of their own languages and cultures.

The architecture of the houses in the region is more varied due, perhaps, to greater economic and cultural differentiation within villages. However, there are basically two major cultural strands noticeable. One is characterised by the style described earlier in east Nepal and the other is what may be called the Lepcha style. The early Nepali settlers had brought their own house-building techniques and these were quite different from the Lepcha techniques. But over the decades a kind of blending of these two styles of architecture can be seen. The houses are of various shapes and sizes but mostly single-storeyed with a living room and a separate kitchen.

The villages also have better infrastructural facilities and are therefore better linked with the market centres. This also means that the economy here is more monetised and there is higher incidence of hired labour than in east Nepal. Crops grown are also more market-oriented than for self-consumption. For instance, growing various kinds of flowers, vegetables and fruits is common. In short, the villagers of Darjeeling and Sikkim have more alternative sources of livelihood than those living in east Nepal.

The region has the three 'Ts'—tea, tourism and trade—none of which is significant in east Nepal. The tea gardens, though over a hundred years old now and many of them sick, are a major employment avenue for the illiterate and semi-literate. Similarly, tourism as an industry is fairly well entrenched. There is also trade in leather, carpets, milk products and bags with neighbouring regions. Such trade is yet to develop in east Nepal.

Finally, Darjeeling and Sikkim are much more advanced in the fields of education, art and literature than east Nepal. This holds true even when we compare the same set of communities or cultures living in the two areas.

Armed with such features, one would imagine that this region would provide leadership to the cultural movements in the entire eastern Himalayas. But this has not occurred. Exposure to various ideas and ideologies, greater interdependence with other cultures, lack of grip over one's traditional beliefs and customs, and the relatively secular state have all been responsible for the lesser enthusiasm and competence of the people of this region than those of Nepal as regards the politics of culture.

2

Kiratas in the Past

The identification of Kiratas in terms of current geographical, cultural and racial distribution in India and its hinterland has been, inevitably perhaps, based almost entirely on Aryan literature such as the epics, the Vedas and the Upanishads. In this regard, the use of historical and archaeological sources of data has been limited, particularly for ancient and medieval times. As a result, there is serious difficulty in ascertaining whether or not the present Kiratas have a traceable descent from those mentioned in the ancient Aryan literature.

The agendum of relooking into the various controversies centering around their origin and identity is still valid. For many cultural organisations of this region, the word 'Kirata' still evokes a sense of being both aboriginal and 'advanced'. It is worthwhile to look into the arguments behind some seemingly innocent theories dealing with their origin and identity, and to reveal the various forms of appropriation of the Kiratas as a race, culture, nation and tribe by the dominant discourse in India as well as Nepal.

Origin

I begin with the etymology of the word 'Kirata'. Suniti Kumar Chatterjee, in his celebrated work, *Kirata-jana-krti*, makes an exhaustive survey of the ancient connotations of the word and those akin to it in the Indo-Aryan languages (1951:17–19). From what he has illustrated, the word 'Kirata' had a negative, sub-human or animal connotation. For instance, in the Vedic as well as other Indo-Aryan literature, this word referred to an ugly man, a wild man, a cruel and mean person, a corn-chandler, a robber, a forester, and the like. This is similar to Leo Kuper's remarks:

> Dehumanization is the most common process in the characterization of subordinate races by a dominant race. It is expressed, in its extreme form, in conceptions of the subject race as animals or demons or objects, and in a less extreme form, in the conception that the subject race is characterized by a falling-off from the fullness of human quality and human dignity (1974:11).

That it is the dominant Other which always defines its subordinate categories is very well brought out by Aloka Parasher in her *Mlechhas in Early India* (1991). But it is perhaps more important to note the (un)conscious borrowing of the dominant discourse by the subjugated. Witness, for instance, the effort of a Kirata scholar, Narad Muni Thulung, to interpret this word. To him, it is derived from two words: *Kira* meaning 'lion', and *ti* meaning 'people', or 'people with lion's nature' (1985:85). Iman Singh Chemjong, a noted Kirata scholar, champions the view that the word 'Kirata' is a "corrupt form of Kiriat, Kiryat or Kirjath which means a fort or town in [the] Moabite language of [the] Mediterranean region" (1966:2). Yet another instance is found in the contention of G. P. Singh, a historian from Manipur University, who considers this word to have possibly originated from *Cireta*, *Cirata* or *Cirayeta* (1990:96). This is the name of a herb which is famous for its bitter taste and high medicinal value, and which is known to be one of the important articles acquired by the Aryans from the Kirata mountain-dwellers.

With regard to the region where they probably originated, Chatterjee locates it "in the mountains, particularly the Himalayas and in the North-eastern areas of India" (1951:16), But Chemjong has a different theory. According to him, the place of their origin is Babylon from where they were driven out by the Hebrews under the leadership of Moses and were forced to migrate towards the east. One of those migrant groups is inferred to have lived in Mesopotamia about 2400 BC, prior to leaving for northern India via northern Persia (1966:3).

This hypothesis is based on the assumption that the Greeks knew them by the name of *Kirhadi* and that they are mentioned in the Old Testament (2 Samuel 15, 18) as a martial tribe during the reign of the Syrian king David in 1049 BC. In support of this, Chemjong also cites Kirata folklore which connects them with the Hazara tribe of Kabul or Golku (Chemjong 1966:5). Bikram Singh Hasrat, a noted historian, is also of the view that the Kiratas migrated from Mesopotamia to northern India and the Himalayan region (1970:xxiv).

G. P. Singh, quoted earlier, argues that "[m]ost of the Kirata tribes of northern and eastern Himalayas were of indigenous region [*sic*]", but, admits that the Kirata regions received waves of migrants who were slowly absorbed into their fold (1990:79–81).

Chemjong's hypothesis, supported by Hasrat, deals with ancient migrations from the West, which probably took place earlier than the coming of the Aryans to India. This is perhaps the reason why Chatterjee, whose sources of information are primarily the Indo-Aryan texts, locates them in the eastern Himalayas and northeastern areas of India. But it is perhaps difficult to support either the migration theory or the indigenous origin theory outside of a specific time frame. They were, perhaps, indigenous in comparison to the Aryans but one cannot be equally sure of a period much earlier than that.

It appears from various historical writings that there was a Kirata substratum in the eastern Himalayas, which absorbed migrants from different directions at different periods in history. It is also indicated that such migrations occurred in trickles: the glaciers on the north and the long malarial terai in the south must have dissuaded many aspirants from migrating to the Himalayas. It is also not difficult to visualise that the indigenous people moved about on account of shifting cultivation, pastoralism and trade.

There is little doubt, however, that the Kiratas are of Mongoloid origin. Chatterjee writes that Indologists agree that the Kiratas have a "non-Aryan" or "Mongoloid" origin (1951:6). This is endorsed by Chemjong too, though he mistakes 'nationalities' for 'races' (1966:4). Other later scholars like Hari Ram Joshi (1985:23) and K. C. Mishra (1987:98) have also reiterated the Mongoloid origin of the Kiratas.

There are, of course, some scholars who disagree. In a widely read book written in Nepali, *Vedma ke Chha?* (1981), Swami Prapannacharya (a Rai) puts forward an antithesis. Drawing extensively from the Vedas, he contends that the Kiratas are of 'Aryan' and not of 'Mongoloid' origin. Though apparently it seems to be a simple case of mistaking 'culture' for 'race', one can trace in his writings a great sense of obligation to show that the Kiratas are as 'advanced' as the Aryans. Having come in close contact with Aryan religious institutions and practitioners in India, he must have felt this sense of responsibility towards his own 'people'. Thus it is, perhaps, not justified to brand him a 'traitor' or a 'stooge of the Aryans', as is occasionally done in some Kirata texts published subsequently.

Here one may refer to an important article on the Aryan identity by A. K. Danda (1992:78–84). After examining the four distinct parameters of their identity—as a physical type, as a spatio-demographic expression, as a philological identity, and as a techno-cultural category—he concludes that "... the Aryans in India, despite their apparent linguistic homogeneity, appear techno-culturally diverse and ethnically heterogeneous" (1992:84).

The burden of Prapannacharya is also shared by G. P. Singh. This is probably why his views about the racial origin of the Kiratas are ambiguous: he occasionally considers them to be of mixed origin and at other times, of pure Aryan origin. For instance, he writes (1990:62) that they were "both of Aryan and non-Aryan extraction" but a little later he says that "after having deeper insight into all the details their Kstriya origin can be proved beyond all doubts" (1990:66). With specific reference to the Tripuri Kiratas, he writes that they belonged to "both Kstriya and Mongoloid stock" and of the Kiratas of ancient Nepal, that they were of "Kstriya origin of Aryan stock" (1990:88).

Prima facie, this ambiguity has arisen out of the conceptual meddling of culture and race, and from the sense of obligation which many Kirata scholars share in proving that they were as advanced as the Aryans. Apart from these two major factors, one should not ignore the ambiguous character of the Aryan texts themselves which not only emanates from the very nature of the language (Pali or Sanskrit) which is susceptible to multiple interpretations but also from the fact that the authors of those texts used different historical, social and cultural sources.

Geographical Spread

The literature on the geographical spread of the ancient Kiratas is rather inconclusive, partly due to the reasons discussed above. While Chatterjee associates them with the northeastern Himalayas, he does not negate the view of Gopal Chandra Praharaj who locates them in "Northern India" nor does he refute Jnanendra Mohan Das who claims that their ancient habitat was "the Eastern Himalayan tracts, including Sikkim and Bhutan, and Manipur and other adjacent tracts, which are exactly the lands of Mongoloid settlement in India" (Chatterjee 1951:18).

With Chemjong, the geography of the Kirata settlement gets further widened. Quoting the *Markendya Purana*, he writes that "the famous seven Kirat[a] kingdoms during the Mahabharata time were Aswa Kut or Kabul, Kulya or Kulu Valley, Matsya or North Bihar, Paundra or Bengal,

Sumer or Assam, Malak or Mlek or Lohit, Kinnaur Kirat[a] or Garhwal and Nepal" (1966:9).

There are others who restrict Kirata settlement to well-defined present-day political boundaries. For instance, Milton Sangma, a noted historian, writes that the word 'Kirata' referred to the "peoples now represented by the Mongoloid group inhabiting different parts of North-East India" (1985:59). Contrast this with the following claim of K. C. Mishra: "Geographically, racially and linguistically they (Kiratas) are identified with the Kirantis or the people of Kiratadesa situated between Dudh-Kosi and Kanki river in east Nepal" (1987:99). These two views, however, appear to be based (rather inadequately) on contemporary racial, cultural and linguistic aspects.

One of the few scholars who has made a meticulous effort to locate the geography of the Kiratas is perhaps G. P. Singh, but even he has found it difficult to assign any particular location to them. For instance, at one point he writes about the Kirata settlements in "the Gangetic plain[s], the valley of Nepal, the hills and mountains of northern, central and eastern Himalayas, Vindhya region, etc." (1990:95) but later he mentions their expansion into "north-western, northern, central (Madhya-desa), eastern, western, northern and greater India" (1990:121). And the 'proof' of such a claim is the fact that the word 'Kirata', or its variants, are found in the various classical texts dealing with those regions. Even when allowance is made for a little sporadic archaeological and other evidence it is difficult to ascertain if the reference is made to the same Kiratas or to an altogether different category of people.

A major reason for this ambiguity is certainly the absence of a clear conception of who the Kiratas were or are. As long as this is so, the question of their geographical spread will remain unresolved. But deciding the space/time framework for conceptualising Kirata identity is not easy. Certain groups of people who are identified as Kiratas or who used to be referred to as such no longer desire this classification whereas others have appropriated and actively propagated it in order to establish their historical antiquity in a given geographical area. For instance, the Meities of Imphal Valley and the Garos of Meghalaya still claim to be of Kirata stock. Those who have disowned this identity are basically people who underwent a process of 'Sanskritisation' during the last couple of centuries and discovered the Kirata identity to be inadequate to represent their changed status. The fact that the Sanskritisation process had established the hegemony of what may be described as the Aryan discourse and relegated the Kirata status to the periphery, both geographically and culturally, must be underlined. Incidentally, such people are recently showing renewed interest in Kirata society and culture. An identity which appeared to be a 'liability' is gradually being appreciated as a 'resource' today.

Consequently, the exercise of identifying the geographical location of the Kiratas at any point of time in history can perhaps never be fully satisfactorily carried out. Even when it is confined to the ancient period there can be no unanimity, because while there may be agreement on when this period ended there may be no agreement on when it began.

Relationship with the Aryans

Any discussion on the Kiratas will remain incomplete without reference to the Aryans because it is essentially the latter who have constructed the former. The Aryan discourse on the Himalayas, which has hitherto remained unchallenged, shows the status of the Kiratas as being subordinated to the Aryans. But it seems that this subjugation was more cultural and discursive rather than political, administrative, or even economic.

The claim of cultural superiority can be traced in numerous Aryan stereotypes existing in their literature. Though these are not a completely valid index for understanding the structural locations of the two categories of people, there is hardly any alternative to this problem. Most Aryan stereotypes about the Kiratas can be translated as 'uncouth', 'unpleasant', 'barbarous' and 'sinful' (Chatterjee 1951:18; Mishra 1987:99). Counter views about the Aryans like 'treacherous' and 'untrustworthy' exist in the oral traditions of the Kiratas. As such, these merely indicate that the Kiratas did not consider the Aryans to be a superior race, but only unfriendly and uncooperative. On the other hand, most Aryan stereotypes seem to indicate that they treated the Kiratas as an inferior race.

In dealing with the Aryan–Kirata relationship a clear paradox is apparent in the orientalism of the texts. Orientalism, according to Said (1978), necessarily presupposes the existence and opposition of two worlds, two geographical areas (or mindscapes, if you like): the privileged term Occident exploring/studying/reconstructing the object of its study—the Orient. What we notice in the oriental texts of the Aryans is, however, "a further division of the Orient (in this case, India and Nepal) in which the received dominant discourse of the West is assimilated without really challenging it and continues to carry forward its hegemony in imposing the same values and weaknesses on their subjects of inquiry which are thereby rendered marginal" (Po'dar and Subba 1991:78).

4

This thesis is substantiated by innumerable instances of the 'othering' of the Kiratas by the Aryans, so well brought out by Parasher (1991). This was possible because the Kiratas, while refusing to fully assimilate with the dominant Indo-Aryan social organisation, were not completely isolated from it either. Thus, if not geographically and historically, at least at the level of discourse, the Aryans represented the Occident and consciously 'othered' the Kiratas, their Orient.

G. P. Singh draws an interesting instance from the *Brahma Purana* (110, 8, 9) which indicates that the Aryan 'othering' was not confined to their texts but was practised by them though the Kiratas resisted such forms of domination. For instance, Singh writes that the "Kiratas, Yamnas, Sakas, Hunas, Khasas, Andhrakas, etc. as mlecchas, were well known for their hostile attitudes towards the class of Brahmanas" (1990:73). This hostility was probably cultural rather than political and economic, though political hostility cannot be ruled out completely.

In the economic field, it appears that the Aryans and Kiratas had trading relationships rather than a clash of interests. It has already been mentioned that the bitter medicinal plant called *Cireta* or *Cirata* was bought by the Aryans in exchange for hides, mats and the like. The *soma* plant was also acquired by the Vedic saints from the Kiratas as they were not allowed to deal with this trade themselves according to *Smrti*, *Manu* and *Yajnavalkya* (Singh 1990:197). But Singh notes that the trade accounts in classical sources are often confusing and sometimes even contradictory (1990:203).

Sources show that the important articles of trade between the Aryans and the Kiratas were cotton, silk, gold, iron, *malbathrum* and so on. But it is not yet clearly established whether silk was bought or sold by the Kiratas. While it is evident that the Assamese Kiratas were expert silk cultivators and weavers in the early centuries of the Christian era, it is likely that as a trade article silk flowed from north to south rather than the other way around (Singh 1990:209–10).

From this brief sketch of the ancient trade between the Kiratas and the Aryans it appears that they had some kind of interdependence. The cultural, ideological and other forms of inequalities between them do not seem to have posed any obstacle to economic transactions.

Kirata Dynasty

The tradition of keeping chronicles of rulers is as old as the writing of history. Such chronicles are an important source of history even today though they do not always meet the standards set by modern historians, particularly after the rise of Subaltern Studies. The native historian today is often not aware of what Perceval Landon realised at the beginning of the present century. Citing a Kirata chronicle, he shows the "unwisdom of applying western scientific tests to the statements of such a chronicle as the Vamshavali..." (Landon 1928/1976:228).

It should first of all be remembered that all the available information on the Kirata dynasty refers to a place called 'Nepal' whose boundaries in earlier times were different from what they are now. Most literature shows that 'Nepal' in ancient times referred to the present-day Kathmandu Valley only, though, according to Chemjong, it was bounded by the Trisuli river to the west and the Tambakoshi river to the east, Chitlang to the south and the glaciers to the north (1966:7). Even if the boundaries suggested by Chemjong are accepted, it is clear that the eastern and western parts of modern Nepal were not part of 'Nepal' earlier.

But even with regard to ancient Nepal, there is no unanimity among scholars about its dynastic history. Opinions also differ over the total number of Kirata rulers between 3102 BC and AD 600. According to some it was 22 and to others 32, whereas Singh considers 29 to be the most plausible figure. Similarly, the total number of years under their rule is found to range from between 1100 to 1500 years. In this regard, Singh makes a safe and rational statement: "they ruled over the valley of Nepal tentatively for one thousand years in both pre- and post- Asokan period" (1990:404).

It may be further noted that almost every scholar has drawn the genealogy of the Kirata rulers from Yalambar [also spelt 'Ilamb' by Padmagiri, 'Yellong' by Kirkpatrick, 'Yalambara' by Wright, 'Yalamba' by Levi and 'Yalambhang' by others] (see Hasrat 1970:xxv). But Chemjong does not seem to agree with this view. According to him, the first Kirata king of central Nepal was Banashur who was conquered and slain by King Bhuktaman. But, after eight generations, when King Bhuvansingh was ruling, a Kirata king of east Nepal called Yalambar slew him in battle and re-established the Kirata dynasty there (Chemjong 1966:6–7).

In short, the available literature provides limited knowledge about the Kirata dynasty in present-day central Nepal. What is certain is that the Kiratas ruled over this part of Nepal for a considerable period of time until they were overthrown by the Licchavis, whose dynasty is fairly well documented.

3

Delineation of the Kirata World

A delineation of the Kirata world is necessary for two reasons. One, the cultural, racial and geographical boundaries of the category 'Kirata' are hazy. And two, it is not possible to understand the world in depth if the social and geographical landscape is not clearly drawn. The term 'eastern Himalayas' covers a wide geographical space including the hill areas of north Bengal, Sikkim, east Nepal, Bhutan, Tibet and Arunachal Pradesh. For the purpose of the present study, the eastern Himalayas refer only to east Nepal, the Darjeeling hills and Sikkim, which are physically, historically and culturally contiguous.

Similarly, the word 'Kirata', which includes a host of Mongoloid peoples living within this region, has been used here as a single expression for three cognate communities called Limbu, Rai (Khambu) and Yakkha. According to Richard English, these three Kirata communities "share common racial and linguistic origins as well as a body of oral tradition which traces common ancestry and identifies the eastern hills as their ancestral homeland" and further that "complementary elements of custom, belief and social organization reinforce a collective identity that is distinct from other ethnic groups, especially the Hindu castes, which have settled the region in large numbers" (English 1983:4).

The People

In early literary accounts, only the Khambus appear to be considered as Kiratas. Colonel Kirkpatrick (IOL 1786-95) suggests that the Limbus, who are taken here as one of the principal Kirata groups, were not considered as 'Kirata' till the beginning of the nineteenth century. Hamilton (1819/1971:53–54), writing on the same period, suggests the same.

Though Brian H. Hodgson (1858) shares this view, he writes that the inclusion of the Limbus and the Yakkhas into the Kirata identity is justified because they "are at all events closely allied races, having essential community of customs and manners with the Kirantis, and they all intermarry, nor probably do the dialects of the Limbus and Yakhas differ much more from the Khwombu [*sic*] tongue, than that tongue now does from itself" (1858:448–49).

It is interesting to note that similar views are expressed by Edward Tuite Dalton in his *Descriptive Ethnology of Bengal* (1872) and by Daniel Wright in his *History of Nepal* published in 1877. Early twentieth century writing, as in Eden Vansittart's *Gurkhas* (1915:96), continues the traditional thinking.

Coming to non-European literature, reference may first be made to the classic work *Kirata-jana-krti* (1951) by Suniti Kumar Chatterjee. He identifies the Limbus, Khambus and the Yakkhas living "on the Indian side of the Himalayas, in Nepal and Sikkim" as Kiratas but his mention of the Khambus and Rais (who are the same group) as separate groups makes his familiarity with the people of the region suspect.

I. S. Chemjong (1966), on the other hand, includes almost all 'Mongoloid' groups of Nepal like the Lepcha, Mangar, Gurung, Tamang, Sunuwar and Hayu under the umbrella of the word 'Kirata'. Though he claims that his definition is based on Kirata chronicles, it is no different from the Vedic or Upanishadic. However, it has been suggested by some scholars that Chemjong chose such a definition as it was better suited to his political aspirations towards a Kirata statehood. This is not unlikely in view of the fact that he did not include other Mongoloid groups living outside Nepal, Darjeeling and Sikkim, such as the Bodo, Garo, Naga, Meitie and the Tripuri.[1]

D. R. Regmi, in *Ancient Nepal*, provides yet another view. According to him, "not all the people in the eastern Himalayas but only two of them, the Khambus and Limbus, are taken as Kiratas" (1969:16). However, he adds that the identification of a "section of Newars" with "the historical Kiratas as their own descendants may not appear far-fetched" (1969:55). Thus, he takes out the Yakkhas and brings in a 'section of Newars'. But he is not the only person to drop the former as they are very often clubbed with the Khambus or Limbus, as the case may be. He is also not the only person to include communities other than the trio of Limbu, Khambu and Yakkha under 'Kirata'. For instance, Northey and Morris write that the Danuwars and Thamis also legitimately claim to be Kirata, but being of mixed origin and of comparatively little importance, they are not taken seriously (1974:215).

None of these scholars has put forward the view that the Khambus alone should be treated as *the* Kiratas. There is, therefore, every reason to believe that the label 'Kirata' was essentially a construct of the Indo-Aryan people who did not have an accurate knowledge of the Limbus and Yakkhas who lived farther east (Regmi 1976b:1).

The British inherited this discourse and made certain interpolations with probably the same level of ignorance as their predecessors—the Indo-Aryans—about the Kiratas.

History

The history of the Kiratas in the region is discussed in this section, in terms of the etymology of Kirata titles, their political history, and the *Kipat* system.

Etymology of Kirata Titles

The Limbus are also known as Tsongs or Chongs in Sikkim, and Yakthungbas when they refer to themselves in the Limbu language. 'Subba' is a popular title among them in Darjeeling and Sikkim, while in Nepal the use of clan names as titles is more common.

The term 'Limbu' literally means 'archer' and, on the authority of Chemjong, this was a name they gave themselves (1966:63). He even goes to the extent of dating this event, which was "[a]fter the partition of this Kirat land of Limbuwan into ten districts", after the sixth century AD (1966:63). However, 'Yakthungba' is a more popular word in Nepal than in Darjeeling, Sikkim and elsewhere though the Limbuwan Mukti Morcha in Nepal is clearly in favour of the word 'Limbu'.

'Yakthungba' is most likely a combination of three Limbu syllables—*yak* or hill, *thum* or place/district, and *ba* (or *pa*) or inhabitant—which together may be translated as 'hill men'. It has many parallels among the tribes of northeast India too. Another version has it that it means 'yak herders' (see Driem 1987:xv). This is not completely implausible because though they are now middle hill dwellers where *yak* (a cross between the bison and cow) is unknown, a section of them belonging to what is called the Lhasa Gotra have legends about their migration from the north, which is a high-altitude, *yak*-populated area.

About 'Chong' or 'Tsong', the *History of Sikkim* by Maharaja Thutob Namgyal and Maharani Yeshi Drolma says that they are "a tribe who revered the Matog Lama as their Guru, followed him from Tsang and settled with him in Sikkim" (1908:21). John Morris also writes that the Lepchas and Bhutias of Bhutan, Sikkim and Nepal called them Chong because they migrated from the "district of Tsong in Tibet" (1933/1985:86). They might have been called so in the early twentieth century but this word has fallen into disuse in Sikkim after their seat in the State Assembly was dereserved in 1974. In Nepal and Darjeeling this term is seldom used by the Limbus.

According to Eden Vansittart, and repeated religiously by all subsequent British writers, the word 'Subba' means 'chief' and it was a title conferred by King Prithivinarayan Shah upon influential Limbus as a conciliatory measure after subjugating them politically. This might have been true of the state-nominated 'Subbas' but the traditional Subbas existed from much earlier times (Adhikari 1984, Dahal 1988). Mention may also be made of the fact that the conferring of such titles was not without strings attached: in order to become a nominated Subba a payment had to be made—of a fee of Rs 52 (which in the Nepali language metaphor refers to the Bahuns) and 60 *muri* of land which amounted to 82,140 square feet—to the state. Thus, conferring titles was a strategy of the Gorkha rulers to gradually usurp land. However, the Kirata landlords do not seem to have been opposed to such titles and rather craved for them at the cost of their communal land being alienated to the high caste Nepalis like the Bahuns and Chhetris.

The Khambus are also called 'Jimdars' though the term 'Rai' is almost universally used as a title by them. Some Limbus in Nepal still refer to the Rais as Khambus. It is not clear how the word 'Khambu' came into being. 'Kham' in the Bantawa language of the Rais, which is most widely spoken and understood among them, means 'land' and it is likely that this word signified 'landlords'. Some trace the origin of this word to the Kham province of Tibet. The people of Kham, called Khambas or Khampas, have an average height of about 1.80 metres whereas the Khambus are shorter, with an average height of about 1.50 metres only. However, it cannot be precluded that a section of them came from Tibet's Kham province.

Similarly, the origin of the word 'Jimdar' is not clear. According to a manuscript it is a synonym of 'Rai', a title of Khambus as well as the Yakkhas (IOL MSS Eur E 295/11). But Kumar Pradhan, a historian from Darjeeling, suspects that it was "derived either from *jamidar* or 'holder of land' or from *jimmadar*, 'functionary with official responsibility' (*jimma*)" (1991:52). In either case, it probably refers to the same thing because it was only zamindars or 'feudal lords' who could be appointed as *jimmadars* or *jimmawals*. Pradhan says that the title 'Rai' "is said to have been conferred on the Khambu chiefs by Prithivinarayan Shah after the Gorkha conquest of Khambuan; but even prior to that the Sena poten(t)ates of Eastern Nepal had referred to them similarly. However, the title which was spelt as Raya was changed to Rai by the Gorkhalis" (1991:52). Significantly, Pradhan does not include the Yakkhas among those who were conferred this title.

Towards the end of the nineteenth century, H. H. Risley wrote that the Yakkas "have no generally recognized honorific titles, though they claim to be addressed as *Dewan* and call themselves Yak Thomba or Yakherders, with reference to the tradition that this was their characteristic occupation before the tribe crossed the Himalaya into Eastern Nepal" (1891/1981:14).

However, it is fairly well known that they had in fact more than one title such as Rai, Subba, Majiya, Jimi and Dewan though the first two titles were also shared by the Khambus and Limbus respectively. That they were also called Yakthungbas has been confirmed by Driem (1987:xix) and Russell (1992:98), though earlier we have seen that Eden Vansittart considered the Yakkhas to be separate from the Yakthungbas or Limbus. The separation between the Limbus and the Yakkhas has become clearer today with the word 'Yakthungba' used only for the former.

The etymology of the words 'Yakkha', 'Majiya', 'Jimi' and 'Dewan' is also unclear. Regarding the first, many still refer to a Vedic *rishi* called *Yaksha* as their primeval ancestor from whom they took the name of their tribe. Majiya and Jimi were titles of offices similar to Rai and Subba—traditional as well as nominated.

Finally, Hanpon makes some interesting observations about the word 'Dewan'. According to him, 'Dewan' is an ethnic label for the Yakkhas but since the southern Lohorung groups in the Ilam and Panchthar districts of east Nepal also claim their language to be 'Dewan' it may be taken as an identity of the 'Limbu-oid' groups who also often call themselves 'Rais' (1991:30). However, in Darjeeling and Sikkim this is used as a synonym of Yakkha only.

Political History

A description of the Kiratas of central Nepal claims that "their power was great and their dominion extensive, reaching possibly at one time to the delta of the Ganges" (Hodgson 1858:447). But most historians have expressed difficulty in linking the ancient Kiratas with those found in east Nepal today. G. P. Singh, for instance, asserts that the Kiratas of east Nepal "did not have any connection with those Kiratas, who were ruling in the valleys of Nepal" (1990: 77). More recently, Kumar Pradhan makes a similar but more guarded remark: "there is nothing to establish any connection between the present Rais and the ancient Kiratas of the Nepal valley" (1991:52).

The westernmost border of the Kiratas in east Nepal was the river Dudh Koshi which is a walkable distance of about four or five days from even the Kathmandu valley. In a historical study of the Nepalese administration, Tulsi Narayan Shrestha (1989), who has dealt with ancient Kirata administration as well, provides many reasons why he assumed Kirata administration in east Nepal to be the same as that in Kathmandu. This is also supported by Chemjong who writes that the ancient jurisdiction of the valley administration extended upto river Tamba Koshi to the east of Kathmandu (1966:7). And, Kumar Pradhan (1991:52) cites a Rai legend claiming that "they came from a land which originally was a lake", which refers to the Kathmandu valley.

The present east Nepal (east of the Arun river) belonged to the Sikkimese kingdom till the end of the eighteenth century, and the Darjeeling district to British India after the middle of the nineteenth century.

Northey and Morris write that the Kiratas occupied "the country right up to the eastern boundary of Nepal. Although the eastern frontier of Nepal is formed by the Singalela ridge, the country east of this, comprising the British district of Darjeeling, is peopled almost entirely by members of the Kiranti race, and large members of them are to be found still further east in the little hill state of Sikkim" (1974:213). Yet, there are many Indian scholars who believe that the Kiratas in Darjeeling and Sikkim are actually migrants from east Nepal. A few more references may be cited here in order to show that they are not all migrants from Nepal.

In the *Darjeeling District Gazetteer*, published in 1907, L. S. S. O'Malley writes: "Beyond a few Lapchas [*sic*] and Limbus with their little clearing in the forests, an occasional raid from Nepal, or a stray visitor from the table-lands of Tibet, the Darjeeling Hills are practically uninhabited" (1907:29). About Sikkim, authoritative texts like the *Himalayan Journals* (1891) by Joseph Hooker and *History of Sikkim* by Thutob Namgyal and Yeshi Drolma have clearly established the early presence of the Limbus there. Fr. Matthias Hermanns has also written that they "occupied the land as far as Sikkim where they were known as the Tsongpa by the Tibetans" (1954:10). It is also perhaps instructive to refer here to a map of "British Sikhim comprising the Darjeeling Hill Territory and two Morung Purgunnahs" drawn by Captain W. S. Sherwille in 1852. At the bottom of this map is the legend that this mountainous 'country' from 1500 to 4000 feet above sea level is "inhabited by a warlike, beardless Mongolian race named LIMBOOS [*sic*]" (IOL 1852 X/1280/I).

But how were the Kirata kingdoms of Chaudandi, Vijaypur and Makwanpur (Chainpur) in east Nepal conquered or subjugated by the Gorkha Prithivinarayan Shah? Ludwig P. Stiller (1973/1975:136–43) and Kumar Pradhan (1991:106–49) describe how Aryan cultural and racial linkages were fully exploited by King Prithivinarayan Shah to conquer or subjugate the Kirata rulers. Racial/cultural awareness was quite widespread among the 'twice-born' castes of Nepal even at that time.

According to Kumar Pradhan the high caste people (Aryans) of east Nepal could never reconcile themselves to the rule of the "beef-eating monsters"—the Kirata rulers. A person called Bangya Basnet (Chhetri) was "specially deputed to win over the high castes to the Gorkha side" (Pradhan 1991:114). He further writes how Trilochan Upadhyaya, the elder brother of Harinanda and the palace priest of the Kirata rulers, had "betrayed his king and rendered similar service to Gorkha in its attempt to capture the terai or Morung" (Pradhan 1991:115).

The military strategy of King Prithivinarayan Shah, based on racial/cultural loyalties, was effective in conquering the Sunuwars of Hither or Wallo Kirant and the Rais of Middle or Majh Kirant. But it was not so easy in the case of the Limbus of Far or Pallo Kirant. Inhabiting the easternmost border of Nepal the Limbus were farther away and better organised, with more commonalities in the dialects they spoke as compared to the Rais. The Sunuwars too had very insignificant dialectical variations within them but they lived quite close to Kathmandu and their numerical strength was never formidable. However, the Limbus were ultimately subjugated. Kumar Pradhan suggests that it was a case of "voluntary submission" in lieu of certain rights and privileges conferred on their chiefs (1991:122).

If this was true, then there could not have been any battle between them and the Gorkhas. However, S. K. Shrestha gives an account of three wars between them and says that in all three the Gorkhas were vanquished by the Limbus (1985:43–44). Further evidence of military confrontations between the two comes from an extract from *Limbu History* written by Jobhan Singh Phago Limbu in 1843. This manuscript was translated in 1962 from Limbu into English by I. S. Chemjong:

> After getting victory over the Khambu land, the Gorkhas with a view to attack the land of the Limbus, crossed river Arun. When the Limbu kings came to know [of] this, they raised their forces and fought a decisive battle

> on the bank of river Sowa [Sabha] and Arun . . . The Gorkhas could not conquer the Limbu land. On the contrary, the Limbus drove back their enemies from their land. But by the frequent arrival of the Gurkha's reinforcements the Limbus kept on fighting for three years . . . They drove them as far back as Dumj(a) . . . Thus the places between Chainpur and Dumja became their battle field. Although the Gurkhas failed to achieve success in their second invasion, they for the third time sent an army to invade Limbuan under the command of Rambhadra Thapa, Magar . . . When such war between the Limbus and the Gurkhas was going on the news reached [the] Sikkim Palace. The Sikkimese king then declared war against the Gurkhas. The Limbus of Yangwarok district of Limbuan, having claimed their nationality as Sikkimese, joined the Lepcha and Bhutia forces of Sikkim. But by this time, the Gurkhas made a treaty with the Limbus; and for a time the Limbu–Gurkha war came to an end (IOL MSS Eur D 537).

Wars or no wars, the fact remains that the Limbus finally accepted the suzerainty of the Gorkha ruler in 1774. The chiefs were conciliated with grants of titles and considerable privileges, which were, however, gradually withdrawn by subsequent Gorkha rulers. The degradation in their political status and esteem, like that of other Kirata groups of east Nepal, can perhaps be better understood with the help of the following section on the *kipat* system.

The *Kipat* System

The *kipat* system is "a form of communal landownership" but with individual rights over a piece of land, which did not include the right to sell it to another 'tribe' or community (Regmi 1976a:87). Lionel Caplan (who did his fieldwork for 13 months in Limbuan) writes: "[E]ach segment of a dispersed patrilineal clan was associated with a particular territory and individual rights to land were established on the basis of membership in such local descent group" (1967:107–08). Thus, it is more precisely the localised clan rather than the community which had authority over *kipat* land.

However, there is some controversy among historians on its origin. For instance, according to Baburam Acharya, a noted historian of Nepal, it was a system introduced first by King Prithivinarayan Shah. He refutes the possibility that it was devised by the kings of the Kirat region (*Regmi Research Collections* (or *RRC*) 6(9) 1974:165).

This is, however, contested by other historians. Mahesh Regmi, for instance, says that this view does not take into consideration the 'communal' character and 'customary origin' of *kipat* land-ownership and the fact that this system was not confined to Nepal. He further says that "only such lands were traditionally recognized as *Kipat* as had been under this form of landownership (communal) during the time of the Sen kings, before the Gorkhali conquest of that region in 1774" (Regmi 1976a:89). This view is also endorsed by Kumar Pradhan (1991:57).

According to I. S. Chemjong, the *kipat* areas were called *Tangsing Khoksing* by the Limbus (1961:56–58). Being the earliest settlers, they were probably the first to clear the forests and start cultivation, after placating the local gods and goddesses.

It is also not yet clear how the word 'kipat' came into being. K. P Bhandari's view is that *kipat* stands for 'ki' or 'kiranti' and 'pat' for 'fallow or barren land' (1959). This interpretation suggests that this word is of Indo-Aryan origin; but if this is so, it is difficult to explain the fact that it has not found a mention in any of the Gorkha chronicles and royal decrees until the time of Ran Bahadur Shah in 1788. Shrestha, on the other hand, argues that this word is derived from the Limbu language in which it means 'revenue-free land' (1985:51).

A part of this confusion is because this system is unduly associated only with the Limbu community. The geographical area demarcated by the Arun and Mechi rivers in east Nepal and traditionally inhabited by the Limbus is often identified as the only *kipat* region but it was by no means so. The list of *kipat*-owning communities is indeed quite long: Limbu, Rai, Yakkha, Tamang, Hayu, Chepang, Baramu, Sunuwar, Danuwar, Kumhal, Pahari, Thami, Sherpa, Majhi and Lepcha (Regmi 1976a:88).

The principal characteristics of this system were:

1. Right to land was determined by one's membership to a patrilineal clan and it was inalienable.
2. It was a possession which was customarily held by the people from the time of their ancestors.
3. It not only included cultivable land but also wastelands and forest areas.
4. Individual ownership to such land was subject to the condition that if a person did not exercise his right for some reason, this right would automatically revert to the clan to which he belonged.
5. Finally, it was tax-free though the homesteads within it were taxable.

Due to various socio-political developments in Nepal since the last quarter of the nineteenth century, this system of land-ownership faced severe crises and it was finally abolished during the 1960s. The recession in this system and the factor(s) responsible for it have been explained below. For the sake of clarity, the *kipat* system in Limbuan and outside it are discussed separately.

a) Kipat in Limbuan: It is perhaps pertinent to start with the royal order addressed to the Limbus by Prithivinarayan Shah in July 1774:

> We hereby pardon [a]ll of your crimes and confirm the customs and traditions, rights and privileges of your country. Join our Bharadars and render them assistance. Take care of the land as you did when it was being ruled over by your own chieftains. Enjoy the land from generation to generation as long as it remains in existence. You are different from the 900,000 Rais, because [their] chieftains are to be displaced, but not you[rs] . . . As mentioned above, remain under your chieftains and enjoy your traditional rights and privileges and your lands. In case we confiscate your land, may our ancestral gods destroy our kingdom. We hereby inscribe this pledge in the copper plate and also issue this royal order and hand it over to our Limbu brethren.
>
> (*Regmi Research Collections*, 6(5) 1974:85.)

Though this order was important in view of the stature of the person who issued it, his descendants did not honour this promise he made to the Limbus. That it was not honoured has become a major cause of the cleavage between the state and its officers, the Tagadharis, and the Limbus (and other Kirata communities of east Nepal).

The order is important on yet another ground. This is an example of what Leo Kuper calls the "objectification" of the subordinate race, by which he refers to a situation "in which a concrete object (copper plate, here) governs the domination, the bonded subject being only the appurtenance of the land, and sinking psychologically to the category of a mere thing, since he is subordinate by virtue of belonging to a thing" (Kuper 1974:14).

Even this 'objectification' of the Limbus would perhaps not have mattered so much if the successors of Prithivinarayan had resisted from devaluing it completely. Caplan writes that they lost no opportunity to reduce the area under *kipat* tenure and at the same time convert these lands to *raikar* (or government land) tenure (1970:56).

Mahesh Regmi seems to justify the circumstances under which this happened. For instance, he says that the *kipat* system deprived the government of both land and revenue, and perhaps more importantly, "prevented the government from establishing effective administrative control over the whole of its territory" (1976a:92). But it should be noted that the 'eating' of Limbu land, as the Limbus put it, was more surreptitious than overt: the documents confirming *kipat* holdings did not specify areas and boundaries: they simply said "lands being cultivated from the time of your ancestors" (Regmi 1976a:94). Hence, it was feasible for a Bahun or Chhetri official to interpret the documents in his favour and encroach upon such lands as he wished.

In 1866, the Nepalese government passed discriminatory legislation allowing the non-Limbus, referring mainly to Bahuns and Chhetris, to convert into *raikar* all such lands which were mortgaged to them by the Limbu owners. It was further provided that such lands, once converted into *raikar*, could not be reconverted into *kipat* even if their original owners repurchased them. Petitions to repeal such discriminatory legislations were made, but such "requests were turned aside by the authorities" (Caplan 1970:56–57, Regmi 1976a:95).

This legislation is said to have resulted in large-scale alienation of *kipat* land, forcing the Limbus to revolt against the state. During this revolt the Bahun and Chhetri castes suffered great losses of life and property. They were practically chased out of the Limbuan though in the Sankhuwa Sabha district, Madi Mulkharka Yakkhas pride themselves for not having indulged in this kind of activity. Their numbers were not enough to do so. Another reason could be the fictive kinship ties binding the Yakkhas and Bahun/Chhetris in this village.

The state was now forced to act and a series of orders were passed between 1901 and 1903 banning the transfer of cultivable lands from Limbus to non-Limbus. But since such orders were not retrospective, *kipat* land that had already been turned into *raikar* land could not be saved. Only about a third of the total cultivable land was left under the *kipat* system by the end of the Rana regime (Caplan 1970:56).

As per the government rule, "any homesteads built or lands brought under cultivation by the Limbus" did not require to be reported to the revenue authorities until the next revenue settlement. But, in practice, the authorities entertained secret reports of such cases from their caste fellows and punished the Limbus by confiscating the lands which were then given away to the informants as a 'reward' (Caplan 1970:58). Caplan also cites an incident which took place in 1913 in which a Chongbung Limbu's land was not only confiscated and given to a Brahman but the former was even ordered to pay a fine of NRs 1,570 by the court (1970:63).

Caplan considers fiscal reasons for converting *kipat* lands into *raikar* as important but contends that "the main concern of the authorities all along has been to establish their own hegemony in east Nepal, and the control and decrease, not to say abolition, of *kipat* tenure, was a priority in effecting such a goal" (1970:59). This would perhaps still be acceptable if the goals were to benefit the state and the means adopted were not casteist. But it was not so. According to Caplan, "The Brahmans have derived the greatest advantages from government *kipat* policy, and so are keen as the prime instruments of that policy. At the expense of the Limbus, they have become the most powerful group in east Nepal society" (1970:60).

b) Kipat outside Limbuan: The official policy towards the *kipat* land outside and within Limbuan was similar, according to Regmi. The difference was in the measures taken by the government to meet its goal and the degree of resistance put up by such communities (1976a:97). With particular reference to Khambuan or the area divided by the Dudh Koshi and Arun rivers—the traditional habitat of the Rais—Regmi writes that when the Rai kingdom was brought under Gorkhali control the Rais were promised "security of life and property" and "succor in all matters". But they were gradually "subjected to various policies that affected their *kipat* land-ownership rights: chief among those policies was the non-recognition of *kipat* rights on wastelands which they reclaimed within the boundaries of their *kipat* holdings. Finally, in 1910, the government of Nepal promulgated orders converging all *kipat* lands in Majhkirat into *raikar*" (1976a:101). However, for another three decades or so, they were not exempted from the *kipat* taxation on the basis of homesteads, though the *kipat* system itself was abolished. It was only in 1940–41 that the government abolished the differential taxation and made it entirely *raikar* (Regmi 1976a:101, English 1983:71–90).

The abolition of the *kipat* tenure meant the end of "communal privilege, regressive taxation, and tenurial insecurity" even to Regmi (1976a:102). Though he is apparently one of the most ardent critics of government policy towards this form of tenure, he seems to justify the end result like very many other intellectuals of Nepal, whose intellectual and racial interests blended perfectly. Here it is worthwhile to remember what Gramsci wrote on the Italian national intellectuals: "The intellectuals are the dominant group's 'deputies' exercising the subaltern functions of social hegemony and political government" (1996:12). How did it matter to them if this meant the very end of the autonomy and cultural identity of the *kipat*-owning peoples?

Present Status of the Kiratas

This section provides a profile of the current numerical, politico-economic and linguistic status of the groups in Darjeeling, Sikkim and Nepal.

Numerical Status

Table X: ***The Regions at a Glance***

Particulars	*Nepal*			*India*	
	Panchthar	*Sankhuwa Sabha*	*Bhojpur*	*Darjeeling*	*Sikkim*
	1981	*1981*	*1981*	*1971*	*1981*
Households	26507	27063	34884	n.a.	n.a.
Population	153746	129414	192689	781777	314999
Male	76585	65525	97295	415124	212624
Female	77161	63889	95394	366653	102375
Literacy (%)	24.0	27.5	23.7	33.1	33.9
Area (sq km)	1241	3480	1507	3255	7096
Population density per sq km	123.9	37.2	127.9	24.0	44.0

Sources: *Tathyank Gatibidhi*, 5(1), 1983–84, pp. 1–2; *Sikkim at a Glance*, 1981, p.1; *District Statistical Handbook: Darjeeling*, 1974, p. A.

Table X shows that the male–female ratio is rather balanced except in Sikkim where it is about 2:1, which is due mainly to the heavy influx of male migrants from Darjeeling and Dooars areas of West Bengal after it became the twenty-second state of India in 1975.

Table XI: ***Districtwise population of Rais and Limbus in Nepal, 1971***

District	*Rai population*	*% to district total*	*Limbu population*	*% to district total*
Jhapa	4775	1.9	6125	2.5
Ilam	19474	16.0	12794	9.2
Panchthar	15829	16.8	n.a.	–
Taplejung	4428	5.2	32396	38.3
Morang	9366	3.1	6734	2.2
Sunsari	11998	5.1	2687	1.2
Dhankuta	19001	17.7	15783	14.7
Terethum	901	0.8	37965	31.8
Bhojpur	29601	15.2	16	0.01
Sankhuwa Sabha	16403	14.4	4121	3.6
Udayapur	14506	12.9	27	0.03
Khotang	42672	26.1	n.a.	–

District	*Rai population*	*% to district total*	*Limbu population*	*% to district total*
Okhaldhunga	13347	10.9	19	0.01
Solokhumbu	26204	24.9	6	–
Nepal	221353	1.5	129234	0.9

Source: *Nepal District Profile*, 1982.

Table XI shows that neither of the two Kirata communities constitutes a numerical majority in any of the districts of Nepal, which speaks volumes in terms of the history of their demographic marginalisation. This is mainly due to migration of non-Kiratas to their age-old habitats, though out-migration of the Kiratas is also partly responsible. Out-migration is certainly less decisive a factor as such migrations are in most cases individual and male oriented whereas the influx of the Bahun, Chhetri and Gurung communities are at the level of the family. It is only in the past few decades that Kirata out-migration has, for economic pursuits, become significant. That they moved away from Nepal later than other marginalised communities is clear from the history of the Nepali diaspora (see Subba 1989).

Politico-economic Status

In *Nepal in Crisis*, Seddon, Blaikie and Cameron write that "the ruling class was identified very largely with the 'high caste' Chhetris and Brahmins, an association that remains close to the present day" (1980:28). They further show that the Hill Brahmans ('Bahuns'), Chhetris and the Newars together constitute 22.8 per cent of the total population of Nepal but the percentage of their officials at or above the level of under-secretary is as high as 92.8 per cent. Other caste/ethnic groups, including the Kiratas, constitute 77.2 per cent of the total population but only 7.2 per cent are officials at this level or above (1980:95). Besides, the caste/ethnic distribution of administrators at the national level is heavily skewed in favour of the Brahmans, Chhetris and Newars, who together constituted 97.5, 100.0 and 90.6 per cent in 1854, 1950 and 1965 respectively. On the other hand, the 'Hill Tribals', who include the Kiratas and Other Mongoloids, have none represented in this category in 1854 and 1950 while their representation in 1965 is a negligible 5.3 per cent (1980:96).

F. H. Gaige shows that the 'Hill Brahmins and Chhetris' constitute 80.5 per cent of senior army officers in 1967 whereas from among the Kiratas only the Rais have 1.1 per cent in this category (1975:167). This is also true of the caste distribution of political representatives from different constituencies of Nepal. For instance, Harka Gurung clearly shows the preponderance of the Brahmans and Chhetris (1992:19–21). Thus it is perhaps quite correct when Seddon *et al.* describe the indigenous people of Nepal as 'subject classes' (1979:20).

But the politico-economic status of the Kiratas in Darjeeling and Sikkim does not appear to be as pitiable as it does in Nepal. A. C. Sinha's work (1983:56–75) and my doctoral study (Subba 1989) do not show such caste-class overlap as we notice in the case of Nepal. This is due to many historical and socio-political reasons. For instance, the economic position of high caste members is not well entrenched in Darjeeling and Sikkim primarily due to their relatively late migration. With rather satisfactory socio-political conditions prevailing for them in Nepal, their compulsions to migrate were less than those of the Mongoloid hill groups who had to bear the brunt of the Tagadhari administration. Further, the power and authority, traditional as well as secular, in Sikkim and Darjeeling were never in the hands of the Nepali high caste and they had little or no scope of influencing the state as in 'Hindu' Nepal.

In this regard, it may be added that the spread of education, initially with the help of missionaries and later by the state, made the Kiratas better equipped to defend themselves from the designs of the Tagadharis than were their brethren in Nepal. But it appears that the Tagadharis have since been gradually consolidating themselves economically and professionally especially in Sikkim where Nar Bahadur Bhandari ruled for about fifteen years without a break and patronised a large number of his caste-brethren. State patronage is important today because, as Paul Brass has said, the state is "itself both a resource and a distributor of resources. It is not an abstraction, but a set of repressive, allocative, and distributive institutions and decision-making bodies" (1985:26).

Linguistic Status

In Nepal, the various linguistic groups were allowed to speak in their own languages but they were prohibited from learning how to read and write—even to the extent of being persecuted by the police if they did so. The state policy on language was such that except Nepali no "other languages should be taught, even optionally, in the primary school because few children will have need for them, [and] they would hinder the teaching of Nepali" (cited in Gaige 1975:108). If they could not learn their own languages at the primary level the question of learning them at higher levels did not arise at all. In any case, the state represented by the Tagadharis had the 'legitimacy' to decide who needed what.

This policy, enacted in the late 1950s, still seems to be the guiding principle because even with the ushering in of 'democracy' the state has made no provisions yet for its various linguistic groups to learn their own languages.

The linguistic groups do not have equal facility over their languages. The Newars in the Valley and the Limbus in the extreme east, for instance, have been largely successful in keeping their spoken language alive whereas the Yakkhas and Rais have more or less lost out. Regional variations in the linguistic capabilities of the same group are discernable. For instance, the Gurungs of west Nepal can speak in their own language very well but those in the east cannot. However, wherever there is a sizable group living in a compact area, such as the Newars in Taksar of Bhojpur district, the linguistic capability is fairly high.

Outside Nepal, it is perhaps the Limbus who have been most successful of all Kirata communities in retaining their language. Their language was even recognised as a state language of Sikkim in 1980. Today the Limbu script and language are taught upto Class XII in about 200 schools. The Rais have no such status despite the fact that they are the single largest community there. Of course, they are beset with considerable linguistic diversity within themselves and do not have a script of their own. But now a new sense of enthusiasm to 'invent' their own script has flowered and, given their resources, they may be able to do something positive in this regard.

The relatively better linguistic status of the Limbus in Nepal is attributed by Michael Hutt to their resistance to learning Nepali. Otherwise, most other languages are fast being replaced by the Nepali language (1986:17).

NOTES

1. R. Keith Sprigg, a renowned linguist who has done significant work on Kirata languages and who knew Chemjong personally while at the School of Oriental and African Studies, London, told me during my fieldwork in Kalimpong that the latter did harbour such ambitions.

4

Internal Organisation of the Kiratas

In the preceding chapters, the word 'Kirata' has been used rather unhesitatingly to represent the Limbus, Khambus or Rais and the Yakkhas, who are concentrated in the contiguous areas of east Nepal, Sikkim and Darjeeling. It is perhaps proper at this juncture to discuss the internal organisation of these communities to see if they justify being constituents of the same 'Kirata nation'.

According to Raymond Firth, an 'organisation' is a concrete and ordered activity which is directed towards politically, economically or socially defined ends. In other words, it is a system of "working arrangements of society" (1954:10). The internal organisation of the Kiratas is discussed here with this definition in mind.

Political Organisation

To begin with, attention may be drawn to H. H. Risley's *The Tribes and Castes of Bengal*, Vol II (1891/1981), in which he refers to the existence of a tribal council among the Limbus. He wrongly calls it *thumthum*; the correct term is *chumlung*.

Chumlung, according to Khagendra Songpangphe, an advisor to Sarva Kirant Chumlung, consists of two Limbu words—*chum* and *lung*—the first connoting 'friends or like-minded persons coming together or assembling', and the second meaning 'to thrash out, reveal, express, or to be concrete like a stone'.[1]

The antiquity of this council can be assessed from the fact that it is mentioned in the *mundhum* (or *muddum* to Rais) recited by their sacred priests called *phegangma* (or *nakchong/mangpa* to Rais). In the *mundhum*, there are references to three ancient *chumlungs* known as Ngamuk Sam, Yeyhang Sam and Yeysam. In this regard, the effort of Martin

Gaenszle (1993) to understand the *muddum* of the Mewahang Rais is commendable, and perhaps similar work should be undertaken on other Kirata populations as well. Spelling it *muddum*, he writes:

> This concept semantically implies a certain unity, both in a spatial as well as in a temporal sense. On the one hand it emphasizes the common root of the oral traditions of the various Kiranti groups in East Nepal, and on the other hand it depicts the tradition as a divine knowledge which has been handed down in a basically unchanged way by a long line of ancestors since times immemorial (1993:117).

However, the concept of *mundhum* is not confined to either east Nepal or the Kiratas. It is also difficult to define it to the satisfaction of all. It is therefore safer to describe what it includes rather than try and define the concept itself. It is a body of oral narratives about the origin of the world, human beings, various plants and animals, customs, traditions, rites of passage, other rituals, agricultural crops, hunting, fishing, and the like. Until recently, it existed purely in oral form recited by priests and a few elderly, scholarly persons. Now several have been textualised.

Coming back to *chumlung*, Chemjong's *Kirat Itihas* (1982), written in Nepali, shows how it has always been an integral part of the Limbu culture and history. The practice of the Limbus meeting at a place and deciding on any important matter seems ancient. This is also evident from the principles of the traditional Kirata administration discussed in the same book (1982:35–36). It appears that no one, not even a king, could take any vital decisions without taking the *chumlung* into confidence. One might cite this instance as evidence of democratic governance among the Kiratas in ancient times. However, it is likely that such discussion took place only among the Limbu landlords whereas the poor and the non-Limbus probably had no representation at all in such councils.

The institution of the *chumlung* suffered a serious setback after the Limbu kings came under the Gorkha rulers. The introduction of state-sponsored statutory bodies to dispense with judicial matters eroded the power and authority of the *chumlung* in Nepal as well as Sikkim. The role of the *chumlung* was further diminished after the introduction of the panchayati raj in the 1960s. In Nepal, this traditional institution often stood in the way of the 'integrationist' principles of the state. It also lost its value gradually because it was an informal or ad hoc council of the chiefs, Subbas and village elders and it had no mass participation.

The *amal* or Subbas' court was a more localised and tangible institution. This court was empowered "with rights to hear cases of a civil nature involving damages not exceeding Rs 100, and with authority to impose fines of upto Rs 25" (Caplan 1970:129). The authority of the Subbas court regarding law and order extended beyond the formal boundaries of its jurisdiction but not beyond what the state thought was the limit.

This court became defunct in the 1920s. According to Caplan, this was mainly due to "the spread of government courts, which usurped many of the functions of the *amal*, and, of course, partly to the fact that the Subbas have lost much of their traditional power" (1970:139). According to Dahal (1988: 99), the characteristics of a traditional Subba were:

1. authority is achieved rather than availed,
2. power or authority is culturally sanctioned, and
3. the traditional Subba is paid in every ceremony/ritual as his customary royalty.

On the role of a traditional Subba in the Athpahariya Rai political organisation, Dahal writes that he "played a major role in the socio-religious life of the Athpahariyas. He was indispensable for carrying out ritual activities or purificatory ceremonies. He had the power to induct non-Athpahariyas into the fold and would also give a new clan name to his inducted member" (1988:98).

It may be stated here that not all Subbas were traditional: some of them were also nominated by the state. Such a Subba was known as *tiruwa Subba*. He could be any wealthy person and was not required to be born into a particular Kirata lineage or clan. Among the Athpahariya Rais, the nominated Subba was "the representative of the state" and the "main channel of state control within the territory" (Dahal 1988:99). Thus he was responsible for gradually extending Nepalese laws into the Limbu, Khambu, Yakkha or other such societies.

Dahal also writes that the traditional Subba was more 'honoured' than the nominated Subba (1988:100). But that the former was not as powerful is indicated by the desire of such Subbas to pay Rs 52 and 60 *muris* of land to the state and be nominated Subbas as well. Hence, the concept of 'Double Subba' emerged in many villages of east Nepal. In any case, the office of the Subba was abolished in 1962, in the wake of the abolition of all forms and symbols of local autonomy and identity in Nepal. At present this title brings no special privileges.

With regard to the Khambus, not much is known about their political organisation. According to McDougal, the local authority among the Kulunge Rais was traditionally in the hands of a clan headman who was later given statutory sanction and called *talukdar*. The *talukdar* was an intermediary between the state and the villagers and also responsible for the "collection and delivery of taxes". There was "no local super-ordinate authority, no village headman over all the various *talukdars*, who were largely autonomous. The *talukdar*s had the legal authority to settle disputes among their *raiti* (non-kipat-holders)" (1973:220).

Ecologically, the population of a village was sparse and spread over about 12 square kilometres beyond which a *talukdar* found it physically impossible to wield his influence. Linguistically, the Rais were, and still are, so diverse that they often repeat a famous cliche *jati Rai uti kura* or 'there are as many languages as there are Rais'. Though they probably became bilingual much before the Limbus did, a superordinate authority over the various *talukdar*s apparently could not develop due to such reasons. McDougal thus aptly remarks that the "effective political unit tended to be the locality" which essentially means a village.

It is uncertain whether this office of the Athpahariyas existed among other Rai groups as well. McDougal's study gives no indication of this. This makes one doubt whether the Athpahariyas are actually Rais. There are broadly two views on their identity: One group believes that they are originally Rais but, having lived for centuries in Limbuan, have adopted the Limbu culture, while the other group argues that they are originally Limbus but due to the administrative title 'Rai' conferred upon them by the state they began to call themselves 'Rais'. There are many other such groups in Nepal such as the Lingthepe and Lohorung whose ethnic identity is not yet confirmed.

The available information is even more scanty on the political organisation of the Yakkhas. Though it is confirmed that they too had a tribal council called *chumlung*, it is difficult to ascertain its details. But if the fact that the Yakkhas' traditional habitat fell within Limbuan is kept in mind and also the fact that they had close physical and cultural interaction with the Limbus, one cannot expect a significantly different Yakkha political organisation.

In fact, cultural and other similarities between the Yakkhas and the Limbus are so prominent that the former often find it difficult to say how they are different from the latter. The illiterate villagers do not appear to be aware of the identity crisis which the educated among them are facing now. To them, their clan identity appears more important than their identity as Yakkhas. Part of the confusion about their ethnic identity is due to the various state-sponsored titles like 'Subba', 'Dewan', 'Jimi' and 'Majiya'. While the last three titles are found only among the Yakkhas, the first is found among the Limbus and Athpahariya Rais as well. Though all these titles essentially refer to administrative offices, they have continued over the years as surnames and created a lot of confusion in the minds of the people as well as those who write about them. Whatever may be the titles held by the Yakkha headmen, their powers and privileges were the same as those of the Subba and *talukdar*. It is also evident that the Yakkhas, like their Limbu and Khambu counterparts, did not have any political organisation worth mentioning beyond the jurisdiction of a village.

To sum up, the political organisation of the Limbus, Khambus and Yakkhas was rather informal and ad hoc except at the village level. It is also perhaps relevant here to remark that it was dominated by the landlord class both in the case of the traditional political organisation as well as the one imposed by the state. It was invariably one such landlord who was the headman, or a member of the council of Subbas or that of the more fluid organisation called *chumlung*. One clearly notices the lack of scope for small farmers, tenants and other agricultural categories to participate in the political organisation at any level.

It is suspected that any conflict in the political organisation was therefore confined to this landlord class. More often than not, conflicts took place between traditional and nominated office-holders over the jurisdiction of their rule. At a more abstract level, the conflict was between social sanction and state sanction between which, history shows, the latter was always victorious especially under non-democratic regimes such as kingship. Even under democratically ruled societies, the sanction of the state is often more powerful than that of the society. This has been more pronounced after the introduction of the statutory panchayati raj in Nepal in 1962, which was 'partyless' till 1990 (Hutt 1991).

This discussion on the political organisation of the Kiratas is closed with a reference to Leach's classic study of the political systems of highland Burma (1954). Not only is the locale of this study close to that of the present study but even the conclusions seem to be similar. Leach finds that "the political organisation of the area has been very unstable" (1954:6).

Economic Organisation

Prior to the arrival of the Tagadharis in east Nepal, it is believed that the Kiratas there practised what is known as shifting cultivation. It is further stated that it was the Tagadharis who "brought with them the technology of the plough and intensified wet rice cultivation technology which was capable of supporting a much higher density of population than the slash and burn cultivation of the Rai and Limbu" (English 1983:28).

But this cannot, perhaps, be taken for granted. The royal decree issued from the Rabdentse Palace by Tensung Namgyal to the Limbus in 1685 (translated by Ringu Tulku, a well known Tibetologist) clearly shows that the Limbus knew terrace cultivation about one hundred years before the 'unification' of Nepal which marked the beginning of more significant Tagadhari migration to east Nepal in the mid-eighteenth century. This decree permits the Limbus to bring the undisputed lands under terrace cultivation (see Dahal 1984:14).

To understand the economic organisation of the Kiratas it is essential to see how the *kipat* system was managed. Campbell has rightly pointed out that petty trade and military service were also important to them (1845:74) but the *kipat* system was for long central to their economic organisation. From one of Caplan's recent works (1991:309), it appears that the economic organisation of the Kiratas also incorporated the non-Limbus. This leads us to another important question: What was the nature of control over land by the Limbus and the non-Limbus? The answer provided by Mahesh Regmi is: "[The] right of Limbu *kipat* owners to redeem their mortgaged *kipat* lands whenever they can has made the tenure of non-Limbu creditors extremely precarious. Such tenurial insecurity discourages efforts to improve the land and raise its productivity" (1976a:102).

Regmi is right regarding the first part of the answer though it is clear that mortgaging of Limbu land was lucrative for the non-Limbus. For instance, Caplan's study shows that 68.2 per cent of *kipat* land was under mortgage of which 82.8 per cent was irrigated and 38.6 per cent formed dry lands (1970:92). The Limbus would not mortgage their land, more so those under irrigation, unless they needed to very badly. This would mean that they would settle for almost any terms and conditions set by the creditors except that ownership of such lands could not be legally transferred until the abolition of the *kipat* system. But Regmi has not given any evidence to show how the 'low' productivity of land in east Nepal is due to tenurial insecurity. Hence his conclusion is based neither on sound logic nor on empirical evidence. Rather ironically, he seems to justify the abolition of the *kipat* system.

It should also be remembered that there were many Limbus who owned non-*kipat* land. They constituted 12.7 per cent of the total Limbu households in the Indreni settlements where Caplan did his fieldwork in 1964–65 (1970:45–53). But it is not clear from Regmi's work if their tenurial insecurity was as high as that of the non-Limbus who seem to be his main concern.

As regards distribution of roles in production, distribution and consumption, it is immaterial to make a distinction between *kipat* and non-*kipat* owning households. The primary source of labour was the family though for certain agricultural operations such as transplanting paddy seedlings, pulverising earthen boulders, carrying cowdung to the field, or threshing paddy, family members alone would not be sufficient. Hence, inter-familial labour exchange took place for certain periods of time in a year. The exchange of labour was of two types: *parma* or direct form of labour exchange between two households, and *hoori* or indirect form of labour exchange involving more than two households. The latter type is also cyclical or circular as members work on each other's land in a cyclical or circular order.

To go a little further, *parma* was normally made up of two persons of the same age and sex and perhaps of the same agrarian category as well. A *hoori*, on the other hand, normally comprises a group of about 10 to 20 individuals belonging to both sexes, various age groups and agrarian categories. Further, a *parma* is normally between the members of the same clan or lineage but a *hoori* may represent many social groups and may even include the Untouchables as it is a sort of neighbourhood group. The only common element between these two types of labour exchange is that there is no question of payment either in cash or in kind except that food and drinks are provided at midday. It is also observed that despite heterogeneity, the *hoori* is a more stable group and both these forms of labour exchange are common among all the three Kirata communities (Subba 1985b).

Now the Limbu economic organisation may be seen from a different angle. Risley's discussion on the Limbu inheritance system shows that their economic organisation was closely interwoven with their political organisation. For instance, he writes that it was the *chumlung* which decided who would inherit how much land, who would be the primary heir and who the secondary heir, and so on. Even the distribution of the *dai jo* land or land gifted to married daughters or sisters, was reportedly the prerogative of this council (1891/1981:12–20). This might have been the case in the late nineteenth century, when Risley collected his data, but this was obviously discontinued by the 1960s when Caplan visited Limbuan and produced his classic on east Nepal.

Yet another dimension of their economic organisation is the system of 'ritual brotherhood', to borrow a phrase from Ferdinand E. Okada (1957).

The practice of two adult males, obviously not related to each other either consanguinally or affinally, entering into a 'ritual brotherhood' is quite common particularly among the traders in the eastern Himalayas. It is called *ingzong* among the Lepchas, *ganye* among the Tibetans and *miteri* among the Nepalis though slight differences can be traced within them (Okada 1957:212). Its significance to their economic organisation may be clear from the way Okada defines it, as a "system which formalizes existing warm interpersonal relationships, encourages the mutual exchange of practical aid in times of stress, and serves to unite individuals of different backgrounds" (1957:212).

On the economic organisation of the Kulunge Rais, McDougal writes that the household is the primary unit. The women shoulder most of the responsibilities within the household as well as outside (1973:210). Here it is pertinent to examine an aspect of their culture which requires its male members to migrate at least once in their lifetime. An adult who has never left his village is compared to the 'frog in the pond' while one who has seen places is acclaimed. But the impulse to migrate cannot perhaps be attributed entirely to their culture: it is also partly accentuated by the absence of employment opportunities within the village except during peak agricultural seasons. Further, being one of the 'martial' groups, they are recruited into armed services in India and elsewhere. The relative affluence of such people further encourages others to migrate. The consequence is a village with very few young males.

McDougal also discusses the importance of trading among them as they acted "as middlemen between the Sherpas to the north and the bazaar towns to the south" (1973:211). But this was not applicable to all Rais. For instance, in Chhinamakhu, the Rais who live in the lower altitudes do carry out limited barter with the Sherpas, Gurungs and Chhetris living in the higher altitudes of the village. But such bartering relates only to agricultural products like maize, paddy and potato, which are used for self-consumption. The goods received from the high-altitude dwellers are not sold in Bhojpur town. However, they sell their domesticated animals and a few cash crops like orange and ginger in this town. This cannot perhaps strictly be labelled as trade because it is not done for profit but in order to buy other essential items like kerosene, salt, mustard oil and clothes for their own use. (This is also true of Dilpa, a neighbouring village.)

The Yakkha economic organisation is not really different from that of the Limbus or Khambus. Like them the Yakkhas were *kipat*-holders inhabiting the ecologically similar middle hills of east Nepal. The only feature of Madi Mulkharka which is absent in the other two villages studied is the existence of some pasture or grazing land called *kharka*. Earlier, there were five such called Mulkharka, Majh Kharka, Tham Kharka, Tundel Kharka and Maimenger Kharka. But now only the last three exist as pasture lands whereas the rest have long been converted into cultivable land or used as building sites. Even the ownership of such lands has changed from lineage to individual ownership. Besides, since the entire area under pasturage is owned by a couple of households in the village, it makes little or no difference to the economic organisation of the village.

Summing up the discussion on the economic organisation of the three Kirata groups, the following observations may be made. One, with the abolition of the *kipat* system, the relevance of lineage or clan to their economic organisation has dwindled if not wiped out completely. The place of lineage or clan seems to have been reduced to the cultural realm only. As a result, the traditional distinction between Kirata and non-Kirata economic organisation characterised by the presence or absence of the communal ownership of land has practically vanished.

Two, the economic organisation of the Kiratas, though still heavily dependent on family labour, incorporates the participation of people who are not members of the clan or lineage to which a piece of land belongs. In this sense, their economic organisation is considerably more 'secularised' today than it was earlier.

Three, with the diversification of economic activities, no matter how limited, economic roles have increased and there are more choices available today. Increased access to information, the spread of education, and infrastructural development have considerably enhanced their capacity to break away from their earlier mono or dual economic roles in the villages.

Finally, the spirit of clan solidarity has apparently been replaced by the spirit of functional interdependence at the neighbourhood level. The chief instrument responsible for effecting this shift is perhaps the growing role of money in the management of economic affairs. Though hired labour is not yet institutionalised among them, there is a growing tendency to use this kind of arrangement among all three Kirata communities.

NOTES

1. Further, the word *chum* may be broken into *chu* and *um* or *m*: the first connoting 'to finish, solve, bury.' and the second 'to ruminate', 'to act' or 'to deal'.

5

Social Organisation of the Kiratas

The social organisation of the Kiratas is discussed here on the basis of family and kinship though these do not exhaust the entire breadth of this concept. Here, caste has not been taken into consideration not because the three Kirata communities are totally outside the caste discourse but because it assumes only a peripheral role. Similarly, religion has been excluded from discussion here but it gets automatically manifested in the ways in which family and kinship operate in these communities.

The Family

In anthropological literature, 'family' is often found equated with 'household', which is defined as "a group of relatives sharing a common kitchen and budget" (Caplan 1970:32). Accordingly, Caplan classifies the Limbu households into 'simple', constituting 90.6 per cent, and 'joint', representing the remaining 9.4 per cent (1970:32–33). Here, our understanding of the situation may be mistaken if what he means by these concepts is not briefly elaborated. A 'simple' household, according to him, is not really a 'nuclear' or 'conjugal' family, nor is a 'joint' household necessarily the 'joint family'. His 'simple' household actually consists of seven different sub-types of which three (Types B, C and D) may, in other contexts, be well considered as 'extended' families. And by 'joint' households, he means "those which include a married couple or widower and at least one of their/his married sons and spouse" (1970:34).

It is perhaps not proper to comment on this as his study was conducted about thirty years ago when the nuclear–joint paradigm might have been important. What is more important to study is how the households or families grow and divide, and relate to each other in the context of other wider groupings. This is examined here on the basis of data collected from the three Kirata villages.

In Yangnam, the ratio between 'conjugal' and 'extended' families is almost 50:50. Due to heavy male out-migration the families tend to become extended until such time as the male adults decide to return home permanently. As long as they are away serving in various countries and professions, their spouses seldom form households of their own and instead continue to be part of their husbands' natal families. This not only provides a sense of security to the women who stay behind but also fulfills other vital functions of the family. The parents can keep a better watch/control over their daughters-in-law and save themselves from any possible scandal in the absence of their sons at home. In some cases, the mother-in-law and daughter-in-law are the only adult members of a family. The daughters-in-law also feel more secure in an established household than in a separate new household of their own. They can also provide additional labour not only in the fields but also in the house itself.

In the extended households, the children have better opportunities for education as well as play, which are more restricted in a conjugal family as more chores are to be performed by a smaller number of family members. The children also enjoy the usual indulgence of their grandparents, which is perhaps why they often stay on with their grandparents when the parents decide to establish a separate household for themselves. When the adult sons are retired from their jobs they almost invariably set up a separate household, which occurs usually due to the lack of freedom which the daughters-in-law experience in their husbands' natal families, though many attribute the cause of such division of households to the proverbial tension and conflict between the daughters-in-law and mothers-in-law. The youngest daughter-in-law, however, cannot escape from the obligation to live with her husband's parents and look after them and other dependants, if any.

The division of a family takes place normally after 15 to 20 years of marriage and lasts only for a decade or so. In the meantime, one of the parents would have died, brothers would have separated, and daughters would have been married off. All these consequently bring about a reunion of the previously divided household. This occurs particularly in the case of the youngest son though it may not necessarily be so. In one instance from Yangnam, a widowed mother opted to stay with her eldest son, whose wife was more hospitable to her than the wives of her other two sons, including the youngest. However, households constituting a very large number of members are rather rare today.

The Limbu families in Yangnam are patrilineal as well as patriarchal, though the latter is not always the case. The patriarchy of Limbu families is sometimes challenged not only by the grown-up sons but even by wives (see Jones and Jones 1976). As a matter of fact, wives taking over as heads of families temporarily is quite common in this village due to the absence of their husbands from home during their employment outside their country. Often, the husbands do not return at all and settle down elsewhere with other women. Others who return may also have wives at the places of their work. Such situations also compel the women to officiate as matriarchs though they continue to hope that their husbands will return one day and relieve them of this responsibility.

The present study in Chhinamakhu, which included 66 Rai families, shows the percentage of conjugal families to be 65.2 and that of the extended type, 34.8 only. One of the reasons why they have a much higher percentage of conjugal families than the Limbus is the fact that most of the land in the village is irrigated and fertile, which has enhanced the sustenance capacity of the village considerably. Since there are numerous perennial streams flowing through the village, irrigation presents no problem and land productivity is higher. This has checked out-migration. The Rais of this village are recruited into the armed forces in India and elsewhere but the menial and unskilled workers are not compelled to migrate as much as in Yangnam, making it possible for more conjugal families to exist in this village. The availability of irrigation facilities and the fertile soil have also made it possible for the villagers to undertake extensive orange and cardamom cultivation and thereby partly overcome their need for a cash income.

Like the Limbus of Yangnam, they are patrilineal and patriarchal but, as McDougal points out, there is "no rigid structure of super-ordination and subordination. Aged parents should be, and normally are, shown respect, but there is no great emphasis on filial piety" (1979:77). He further writes that "[s]omewhat greater liberties may be taken with a grandparent" (1979:77).

Regarding filial piety, no generalisation can perhaps be made. The daughters generally evince more of it than the sons and generally take great care of their parents even after their marriage. The love for *maita ghar* (or the natal family) is never lost and daughters are always happy to be back. One woman in Chhinamakhu said: "I deliberately picked a quarrel with my husband so that I could come and stay with my mother for some days. I was dreaming bad dreams about her and my husband was not letting me come here on this or that plea."

Sons, on the other hand, are known to have not only ill-treated their parents but even assaulted them on occasion. In Tanek village of Kalimpong, there are stories about one Mani Subba beating his maternal grandfather, his sister and even his mother in a state of inebriation. In January 1997, his mother sought support from relatives to hold a panchayat so that her son could be properly chastised. Women have been heard to say that a *chora* is *mora* meaning 'a son is a devil' but this is never said of girls.

Among the Yakkhas of Madi Mulkharka, the percentage of extended households is much higher (68.2). This may once again be explained in terms of the sustenance capacity of their village. The Yakkhas are not only the earliest inhabitants of the village, they are still the largest landholders. Though the land is not as fertile as in Chhinamakhu, the average landholding size among the Yakkhas is much bigger than among other castes/communities in the village. Hence it is possible for them to sustain a relatively larger household than other communities. Another reason for extension of families among them is the out-migration of their adult males.

One typical feature of the Yakkha family which is rare among the other two Kirata communities is the high occurrence of non-Yakkha wives. Due to a relatively smaller population distributed among a limited number of clans, most Yakkha families of the village are consanguinally related. Clan exogamy does not permit them to look for spouses from within their own community. This compels them to seek spouses outside their community and the most natural choice, due to close cultural ties, is the Limbu community.

Apart from this aspect of the Yakkha family, there is hardly any other ground on which it differs from that obtaining in Yangnam or Chhinamakhu. Not only are the various roles assigned to various members of the household the same but even the norms and values which guide the actual performance of such roles are similar. The ratio of conjugal-extended families varies slightly across the three Kirata communities but such a variation may even be found across the villages inhabited by the members of the same community. Authority is formally vested in the hands of the eldest male member of the household but in actual situations it may be, at least temporarily, exercised by any eldest member. Even the joking and avoidance relationships are similar among the three Kirata communities.

Among the Kiratas, every family worships certain deities which belong to the male heads and certain others which belong to their wives.

The deities which belong to the wives are seldom worshipped inside the house, which indicates that their membership in the family is never total. For instance, the married women are not allowed to visit the room where patrilineal clan deities are housed or worshipped, particularly so in the case of the Rais.

In recent years, occupation is gradually assuming a more important status than the traditional values based on age and sex. A serviceman sleeps on a wooden cot, wears better clothes than other members of his family, and gets to eat better food as well. There is often very naked discrimination in the family between employed and unemployed sons. At times, the employed sons enjoy a status higher than even that of their fathers. And, the status of males is by and large higher than that of the female members of a family.

Kinship

Risley was perhaps the first to draw our attention to the kinship organisation of the Limbus. According to him, they are "divided into thirteen exogamous sub-tribes, each of which is again broken up into a number of exogamous septs. The names of the septs are extremely curious. Two or three at the most are totemistic, a few are local or territorial, and one only is eponymous" (1891/1981:16).

The question of 'thirteen' exogamous sub-tribes of the Limbus is, however, debatable today. Some Limbus consider these thirteen sub-tribes as 'original' Limbu clans, rendering other clans a lower status by virtue of their being considered to have been incorporated later. But the more important question here, particularly from the point of view of kinship, is whether or not the Kirata clans were territorial entities whose members maintained 'exogamy' later. Even today, when two Kiratas of the same locality or district in Nepal meet in Darjeeling and Sikkim they spontaneously begin to treat each other as primary kins, and some even enter into *miteri* or fictive kinship if they are unaware of the exact relationship that existed before. Thus the sense of territorial exogamy is quite strong even today in east Nepal. But this is probably an extension of the concept of clan exogamy itself. Such extensions must have been necessitated by a sense of insecurity in an alien place of migration. But the fact that such ties are very selective and not necessarily based on the place of origin indicates that fictive ties also fulfil purposes other than the sense of mutual security.

There are quite unambiguous evidences to show that the Limbuan had thirteen 'thums' or districts. It is probable that the names of the dominant clans living there became the names of the districts subsequently and even a sense of territorial exogamy was developed. This is also indicated by the fact that the earlier marital partners used to be from far away, another district, or at least across a major river. This is, however, a phenomenon which is not very common among the Rais who emphasise *pachha* or lineage exogamy rather than clan exogamy.

In this context, it is interesting to note that John Morris (1933/1985: 92–100) has a list of 56 clans which are further subdivided into as many as 513 'kindreds' by which he probably meant 'lineages', though there is a basic difference between the two: a 'lineage' necessarily consists of a group with a common ancestor (male or female) but a 'kindred' need not have one such ancestor. He has also named certain groups under 'clan' as well as 'kindred' besides mentioning certain Yakkha clans as Limbu kindreds. Examples of the first type are Lingden, Thebe, Papo, Nembhang, Thegim and Loksum, and of the latter, Lingkha and Musahang. Morris has also made the mistake of listing the same kindred under more than one clan, such as Chabegou (now Jabegou) under Thebe as well as Thegim. Finally, what he calls 'clan' (like Panchthar, Tambar Khola, Phedap, Charkhola and Athrai) are actually territorial entities each representing a number of clans. It may be added here that the Limbus enjoy tracing elaborate kinship networks horizontally as well as vertically.[1]

Limbu descent is traced patrilineally and the rule of inheritance is male ultimogeniture with regard to immovable property and female equigeniture about movable properties. Immovable property here refers to land and house, while movable property refers to cattle, gold/silver ornaments, brass or copper utensils, clothes, and so on. Besides governing the rules of inheritance and marriage, descent also plays other important roles in the villages: it is one of the sources of prestige and status as much as it is a subject of ridicule. While it sometimes binds a number of otherwise quarrelling households into a relationship of mutual obligation, it can itself be a potential source of conflict at other times. One of the most important roles it has in Limbu society is that it provides 'legitimacy' to an offspring, whether male or female. But its value seems to be appreciated only by those whose 'legitimacy' is questionable in the eyes of the villagers.

Adoption of non-Limbus into a Limbu clan is still practised though it is a privilege not normally extended to the Tagadharis or Untouchables. A person of non-Limbu patrilineage wanting to adopt a Limbu clan is first advised by the village elders to organise a feast on a particular day. On that day, the villagers gather and in their presence a *phedangma* or any senior member of the clan asks the applicant to touch a stone and a bunch of evergreen grass called *dubo* in Nepali (*Cynadon dactylon*). Then the priest or the officiating person proclaims three times that the person has become a Limbu and indicates who his/her *thar* will be. In response, the people gathered acknowledge this three times (by saying 'yes' or "*O Row*"). This ceremony is followed by a feast symbolically cooked by him/her. After that s/he is taken in as a member of the clan. Similar practices also exist among the other two Kirata communities of the region as well as other tribes of northeast India.

Finally, a word about 'fictive kinship', to borrow a phrase from Prindle (1975). The descendants of such fictive kins cannot intermarry for four generations, which is also the degree of prohibition maintained on the mother's side. But it may be pointed out that such ritual brothers and sisters have no claim over inheritance of property, movable or immovable. However, mourning on the death of such a relative is observed for a day by not consuming salt, oil, or meat and abstaining from merry-making. It is precisely because such a kinship is free from property relations that it is always the best: fictive kins never quarrel, accuse or abuse each other, and are always ready to help each other.

Unlike the Limbus who use the same word—*thar*—for both clan and lineage, the Khambus have separate words for the two—*thar* and *pachha*—respectively. In day-to-day conversation, however, the only word they use is *pachcha*. Lineage is probably of more significance to them than it is for the Limbus.

An indication of this is also found in McDougal's emphasis on the phenomenon of 'clan-fission' which, according to him, is "precipitated by an intra-clan marriage" (1973:206). In spite of the anthropological difference between clan and lineage, this is sociologically not significant. The present study in Chhinamakhu shows that when 'Khambu' is used to refer to the tribe or community, then Kulunge becomes a clan and Tamangchha, Thimra, Morokha and Wadiri become lineages. But clans like Ishara, Khamtu, Charghare and Kangmang are sometimes written as *thar* and at other times as *pachha*. This indicates that the boundaries between clan and lineage are not really static or fixed in their society. Further it was often not possible on the part of all *pachha* members to demonstrate their descent from a common ancestor, in the strict use of the word 'lineage'.

In Chhinamakhu, migration is more important than intra-clan marriage in effecting clan-fission. When a Rai migrates from one place to another, he is referred to by the name of his place of origin and not by the name of his *thar* or *pachha*. Thus, every time he migrates he gives birth to a new *pachha* and makes it theoretically possible for intra-clan marriages to take place. Even otherwise, *pachha* is more important than *thar* in the maintenance of exogamy within a group. This is perhaps one characteristic of the Rais which is different from that of the Yakkhas who emphasise *thar*.

John Morris provides a list of 72 clans which, however, includes the Yakkha clans too. These 72 clans are further subdivided into 1090 kindreds, including eighty kindreds of the Yakkha group (1933/1985: 103–15). But as in the case of the Limbus, this list is not quite correct as the same kindreds are listed under a number of clans while other kindreds are listed as clans by themselves. Even Khaling and Khalinge, which are the same clan, are listed separately. Compared to this, the list provided by Tirtharaj Mukarung Rai is shorter and more accurate. His list contains 15 *thars*, which, however, include the Yakkha clans too. These 15 *thars* are distributed over 345 *pachhas*, including 13 belonging to the Yakkhas (Rai 1992:4–8). But if we exclude those which belong to the Yakkhas, the list is perhaps fairly accurate.

An interesting aspect of Rai kinship structure is that a single clan or a number of clans belong to a particular *samait*, which represents brother and sister together as ancestors. Thus, even if *thar* or *pachha* are different, the individuals may belong to the same *samait*, in which case they cannot intermarry and they have to observe mourning in case of the death of one of the *samait* members. The various *samaits* and the *thars/pachhas* which belong to them are shown in Table XII.

Table XII: *Samait and Thar/Pachha in Chhinamakhu*

Samait	*Thar/Pachha*
Basuri-Yumitma	Yuongchen
Begsuppa-Begsupma	Kwoyu, Bayangi
Busuru-Wachchama	Chamling
Changchayupa-Chenkhama	Khamtu, Khimdung, Siptungkha, Rupabung
Chenkhapa-Chenkhama	Khamyongkha
Chikita-Parengma	Thulung
Chimikpa-Chimikma	Mangpahang
Chyangchamu-Chenkhama	Khamtu, Awaicha, Huongchen, Ruchenbung
Dedebungchuyoungpa-~ma	Chamling
Disimi-Begsupma	Kulunge
Khasekpa-Sirungma	Thulunge
Nachhapa-Nachhama	Dibuhang
Rukkupasnasmi-Yokma	Sotange

Source: Fieldwork, 1992–93

For reasons best known to themselves, the scholars writing on the Rais (see, for example, Allen 1987, Barnouw 1955, Toba 1992) have paid little or no attention to the *samait*. It may be worthwhile to dwell briefly on the *samait* in view of the ambiguity of its meaning and significance to the kinship structure. In fact, the Rais of Darjeeling and Sikkim have little or no idea about it. Even in Chhinamakhu, which is supposed to be one of the cultural preserves of the Rais, people with a clear idea about it are hard to find. Even a *mangpa* or *nakchhong* (priest) often appeared equally ignorant about its kinship or social significance.

Prima facie, the importance of the *samait* seems to be the following: *(i)* it is essential to pronounce the *samait* of the groom and the bride at the time of marriage; *(ii)* the *samait* of a deceased person must be pronounced when the funeral procession returns to the house of the deceased; and *(iii)* it is related to the *kul deota* or ancestoral deity. On further inquiry, it is learnt that the paired structure of the *samait* represents bi-sexual phratry clans, drawing ancestry from primeval brothers and sisters.

McDougal's study throws some light on the economics of reciprocity based on this structure. He uses the term *samlome* but there is no doubt that he is referring to the *samait*. According to him, the brother pays a fee called *mauks paisa* of four paise to his sister's husband when she is married and continues to do so every time a woman of her clan is married until the third generation of her children arrives or as long as the siblings are alive, whichever is earlier. In return, the married sister pays a counter fee called *sibalo paisa*, which is the subscription money for flags of commemoration for the deceased ancestors in her natal clan. She continues to do this as long as she is alive though it is not every time some one dies in her clan that she has to pay this symbolic money: it may even be paid by her younger sisters (1979:82–83, 146). According to McDougal, such a relationship "may be seen as a structural extension of the bond between brother and sister, an extension on the one hand to the entire group of the brother, and on the other to the descendants of the sister in the male line" (1979:147).

Further, the brother–sister relationship does not end with their marriages. Rather it is strengthened by a reciprocal ritual obligation between them. Thus it is not surprising to find a sort of procrastinated nato-locality of the married sisters among the Rais. For instance, McDougal writes that the "newly married female continues to live in her natal home; even after she joins her husband she pays very frequent visits to her natal home, facilitated by the fact that the great majority of marriages take place within the locality, and usually within the village" (1979:83).

The particular instance of *sibalo paisa* payment in the Rai social organisation indicates a fair possibility that they were influenced by Buddhism in the past. Their oral tradition also suggests that they originally came from the north, from a region known as Solo Khumbu, which falls more in the cultural territory of Buddhist Tibet than that of Hindu Nepal. But after years of migration to the middle hills of Nepal and elsewhere such as Darjeeling and Sikkim such traces of Buddhist influence seem to exist only in such forms as the payment of *sibalo paisa*. The culture of erecting memorial stones slabs may of course be considered as an adaptation of commemoration flags.

Like the other two Kirata groups, the Yakkhas are divided into a number of clans like Ulumbang, Kirenge, Kongren, Koyumba, Chhala, Phatlunghang, Nouwa, Yopaliba, Langchawa, Lingkha, Limbukhim, Hohongwa and Sambehang (T. R. Rai 1992:8). This list is, however, not complete. For instance, in Madi Mulkharka, there are the following additional clans: Khamyong, Makhra, Pinuhang, Musahang and Koyonga, and in Tamaphok, where Russell did his fieldwork (1992), Samyehang is also mentioned, though Sambehang and Samyehang must be the same clan.

What is interesting to note here is that except Pinuhang and Musahang, which are the lineages of the Dewan clan, the other clans are further subdivided into named lineages. Of course, many Yakkhas are confused about the ethnic identity of the Dewans themselves. The Dewans, according to some, are not Yakkhas. For instance, Sal Bahadur Dewan of Ward No 7, Madi Mulkharka village, said: "Dewan and Yakkha are not the same. Only Majiyas are Yakkhas. Dewans are Rais." But in Darjeeling and Sikkim, the Yakkhas are known only by their title 'Dewan'. This confusion must have arisen as a result of the state policy of granting both 'Rai' and 'Dewan' titles to the Yakkhas of Sankhuwa Sabha district and there is no reason to believe that the Dewans are not Yakkhas.

Despite great cultural similarities between the Yakkhas and Limbus the kinship structure of the former is closer to that of the Rais than of the Limbus. For instance, the Yakkhas too have a paired ancestry called *sameling*, which is in no way different from the *samait* of the Rais; even the names are similar. However, the Yakkhas seem to have moved farther away from their tradition than the Rais have. This is substantiated by the fact that there are very few among them who can state their *sameling* names. With the erosion of their language the knowledge of their *samelings* has also faded. One old Yakkha remarked pessimistically: "Unless we have a renaissance there will be none after twenty years who can tell you about what you are asking. Even our priests will be of no help because they are mostly Limbus." Twenty years may be an underestimation but his final forecast may well be right.

There are many reasons for their cultural decadence. One important reason is their limited number which, when faced with their rules of marriage, makes them marry outside their community and dilutes their traditional customs and habits. Another important reason is that their traditional habitat falls within Limbuan and they have moved closer towards the Limbu culture. For instance, they strictly observe a typical Limbu cultural rite called *saimundri*. Like the Limbus, the Yakkhas consider it necessary to complete this rite before the death of the married sister. *Saimundri* is essentially a bond between a brother and a sister, which, if not severed with a formal rite, will make it obligatory on the part of the brother to perform all the funeral rites of the deceased sister no matter where she is deceased. Thus, the Limbu kinship relationship between two primary kins of the opposite sex formally ends with the observance of the *saimundri* rite which normally takes place when the bridal party returns after marriage at the groom's house whereas *samait* or *sameling* relationships continue over generations. But more importantly the *saimundri* has no relationship with ancestor worship nor does it have any significance at the time of marriage and death.

The entry of the *saimundri* culture into Yakkha society was not only easy but also natural. This is essentially a relationship of mutual obligation between brothers and sisters. When a Limbu woman is married to a Yakkha man, she would obviously like this ritual to be observed so that her brothers have no obligation in case of her death in a Yakkha village. As a Limbu woman, she would also want her daughter by a Yakkha husband to follow the same; the Yakkha daughter would insist on this because she lives within the same belief system. Further, the Yakkha girl is often married to a Limbu man and cannot escape from the influence of the Limbu culture in either case.

The Yakkhas of Madi Mulkharka are divided into six clans but in terms of marital options there is little room within the village because the various Yakkha clans have now grown as a single exogamous unit. Almost every clan has had to bring spouses from the Limbu community in particular. For marital alliance, the Limbu community is the most obvious choice due to cultural proximity between these two communities. The *miteri* relationship with the Bahun, Chhetri and Gurung castes/communities prevent the Yakkhas from entering into marital alliances with them. The *miteri* relationship with these numerically important castes/communities has made it possible for the Yakkhas to remain politically dominant despite their being numerically rather insignificant. The Pradhan Panch and Upa-Pradhan Panch are both Yakkhas and they hold a lot of influence over the villagers. Some attribute their political dominance to the charisma of one Man Bahadur Majiya, who is not only the existing *jimmawal* but also a living legend. But the wider kinship network based on 'ritual brotherhood' is certainly an important factor behind the Yakkhas' political success in the village. Such fictive ties are often two or three generations old and are reportedly made at the initiative of the non-Yakkha castes/communities. But now this has paid rich dividends to the Yakkhas whose political supremacy would otherwise not hold in the village.

The discussion on the social organisation of the three Kirata communities can be summed up with the following observations. First, the number of extended families, though varying across villages and communities, is rather high. This has been mainly due to the out-migration of the adult males in search of various occupations, making it difficult for the conjugal families to thrive on their own. For instance, the cultural conditioning of the people in the Nepalese middle hills is such that they want to build *pucca* houses made of stone and mud and rising two or three storeys high. The raw materials required for the construction of such houses are locally available. The neighbours and relatives also contribute in terms of labour and raw materials. Yet, it is an expensive affair. The income of an ordinary farmer or a low-grade serviceman is not enough to construct such a house.

Second, descent is traced patrilineally in all three Kirata communities but authority over the family members and property is not necessarily in the hands of the eldest male member. Most conjugal families are under the control of the wives as their husbands are away from home for reasons of employment elsewhere. In many extended families, the authority often lies with the women, specially if they are widows. Even in male-headed families, the women often decide what crops to grow, when to sow the seeds, what to cook, and so on. The men, wherever present, would often have lived away from home for very many years and lost touch with family affairs, which gives their women the scope to make decisions. In some cases, the men are so addicted to alcohol that they have lost all credibility in the society and the neighbours approach the women rather than the men for various purposes.

Third, there is no strict division of labour in the management of either the household chores or the land. In most cases, the women do everything except ploughing, repairing the terrace walls, thatching, or lopping the branches of tall trees. They cook, fetch water, collect fodder for cattle, prepare firewood for cooking, sweep and daub the house, and undertake various jobs in the field as well. It is they who manage the house, look after the children, pound paddy, grind the maize, take care of the visitors and guests, and so on.

Fourth, the family is where two (occasionally three or four) clans actually meet, interact and strengthen their bonds. The husband and wife try and protect the prestige of their respective clans/villages as far as possible. They are not only just husband and wife but also representatives/ambassadors of their respective clans and villages.

Fifth, the rules of joking and avoidance relationships are found better exhibited in extended than in conjugal families. The parents-in-law avoid the sons- or daughters-in-law and the elder brothers and the wives of younger brothers avoid one another. But there is a joking relationship between a younger brother and his elder brother's wife or between him and her younger sisters. The joking relationship involves all those who are called *kutumbas* meaning those between whom sexual relationship is possible.

Finally, a word about kinship terminology. Though kinship terminology is predominantly descriptive, classificatory kinship terms do exist. The extent of descriptive or classificatory kinship terms varies from one Kirata community to another but due to the all-pervading influence of the Nepali language in both Nepal and Darjeeling or Sikkim there is a great deal of homogenisation in this regard. There also appears to be a new fashion of using wrong kinship terms such as addressing a son as 'brother' or a daughter as 'sister'.

The internal organisation of the Kirata communities in the eastern Himalayas is rather complex and no clear pattern is discernible. Their political and economic organisations are comparatively less complex than their social organisation. Despite many differences in the internal organisation of the three Kirata communities they can be taken as a common 'nation' for no nation is internally homogenous. Differences can be actually traced even within a clan, caste, or community. Most importantly, the three Kirata communities believe that they are 'Kiratas'.

NOTES

1. Every Limbu house that I visited asked me to present my credentials not in terms of who I was, what my occupation was, or where I came from but in terms of which clan or lineage I belonged to. They would just take a few minutes to place exactly where I fitted into the kinship structure of the village. Even the Bahuns of Yangnam and Madi Mulkharka were able to do this.

6

Kiratas and Other Social Categories

This chapter comprises a discussion of the subjective as well as objective similarities and differences, bridges and gaps, interdependence and cleavages between the Kiratas and other social categories in the eastern Himalayas. The social categories referred to here are the Tagadharis, the Other Mongoloids and the Untouchables. The discussion is based on cultural and socio-economic parameters.

Kiratas and Tagadharis

The Kirata–Tagadhari relationship is the most important of all in the region under study. They have lived side by side for over two centuries now. Those who left Nepal and settled elsewhere such as in Darjeeling, Sikkim and other parts of India intermingled more actively. Their migrant status, common place of origin, the bond established by the Nepali language, and a common challenge thrown by the host societies were all responsible for less sharply defined boundaries between the disaspora communities. On the other hand, the national policy of integrating the various ethnic groups by Nepal resulted in more sharply defined boundaries between the communities in that country. While this is broadly accepted by scholars working in the eastern Himalayas, English writes:

> Inasmuch as Brahman and Chetri (*sic*) have occupied and continue to occupy positions of privilege in the overarching administrative hierarchy of the country, it is understandable that indigenous populations throughout the hills have largely been acculturated to the fundamental principles of Hindu caste society and have been incorporated into that society in positions of much less privilege (1983:42).

Even before the rise of the 'House of Gorkhas' in Nepal in the mid-eighteenth century, the Kiratas were not totally isolated, though the Kirata–Tagadhari interrelationship definitely assumed more significance after that. The new decisive factor was the state which played an active role in trying to bridge the gap between them, not only linguistically but also culturally and otherwise.

Cultural Relations

On the basis of his pioneering study on the relationship between the Limbus and the Bahuns of Ilam district, east Nepal, Caplan writes that they, among others, "enjoy a set of convictions regarding certain forms of divination associated mainly with illness, and share a common pool of ritual specialists for this purpose" (1970:65). To this one can add the common rituals, festivals, sacred calendar, ritual space, deities, gods and goddesses. Even fasting, non-alcoholism and vegetarianism are a part of the Aryan values adopted by many Kiratas now. Some Tagadharis, on the other hand, have abandoned these values and accepted those which are traditionally considered as Kirata habits such as alcoholism, non-vegetarianism, and the like.

B. P. Upreti (1976:47–70), in an autobiographical article on Limbuan, or 'the land of the Limbus', shows how the Bahuns and Limbus have undergone significant cultural changes, especially after the 1950s. He provides a number of examples to establish his view that if the Limbus have been greatly Hinduised, the Bahuns are not less Limbuised, and there is a marked convergence of these two groups towards secular values (also see Upreti 1975).

Upreti's is, however, not an isolated view in Nepal. As a matter of fact, most writings of the mainstream scholars of Nepal like C. M. Bandhu (1989), Dilli Ram Dahal (1979) and Prayag Raj Sharma (1978, 1986) fall into this category. They have argued that the Tagadharis and Kiratas have lived in close interaction for ages and have borrowed considerably from each other. This cannot be denied but one of them has specially cited Lionel Caplan's work as an example of how western anthropologists have ignored the interdependence and emphasised Limbu–Bahun differences and conflicts (see Dahal 1996). Kuper writes: "the shared elements of culture may suddenly become significant, when the power of the dominant race is seriously threatened" (1974:17). The mainstream scholars of Nepal carry what may be described as the 'Aryan burden'; the burden of legitimising the state and justifying that the migration of the Aryans into the Kirata or Other Mongoloid habitats was legitimate and had no negative consequences whatsoever for the indigenous peoples.

Caplan is not entirely correct when he says that "whereas Brahmans worship the universal Hindu pantheon, Limbus worship, by means of blood sacrifice, a host of deities which have no place in traditional Hindu belief" and that the courtyard of a Limbu "will not contain a shrine for the worship of a Hindu deity. Nor do Limbus follow the Brahmanic practice of propitiating an ancestral god (*kul deota*)" (1970:66). Limbus also worship the "universal Hindu pantheon" and the Bahuns worship a host of local deities which have "no place in traditional Hindu belief". Further, Caplan gives us the mistaken impression that the Limbus do not propitiate the ancestral god, though he is right in pointing out that it is not done in the manner the Bahuns do it by "setting aside a special place of worship" within their home. This Brahmanic practice of propitiating the ancestral god is, however, found among the Rais as well.

Caplan also draws important distinctions between the Bahuns and the Limbus in the spheres of food rituals, mourning practices, marriage practices and the "pleasure complex" (1970:66–69). But these distinctions are more of degree than kind, and this degree varies considerably amongst the Limbus as well as it does amongst the Brahmans.

Due to a relatively longer interaction between the Bahuns on the one hand and the Rais and Yakkhas on the other, the cultural distinctions between them are less sharply defined. But this is more apparent than real, as illustrated by McDougal's study on the Rais. He writes that "... in those areas where the high caste Hindus settled in greatest numbers, many Rais adopted some of the superficial trappings of Hinduism and certain of the minimal ritual observances, gave up eating beef, and, at least outwardly, accepted the validity of the hierarchy of ritual purity which relegated them to inferior status. Others, however, especially those living in the higher and more remote areas, mainly in the north, have remained little affected by Hinduism..." (1979:11). Such heterogeneity within the Rai community is true of Nepal where they are spread over a vast geographical area but in Darjeeling and Sikkim there is a great deal of homogeneity within the community. Hindu influence is more significant in the latter region than in Hindu Nepal itself. Whereas the Limbus in Darjeeling and Sikkim generally abstain from inviting Bahun priests for their *rites de passage*, the Rais patronise these priests regularly. They are not only more Hinduised but also more Nepalicised. They have completely switched over to the Indo-Aryan Nepali language and contributed to the growth and development of art, literature and music in the region.

The only full-fledged study of the Yakkhas is that of Andrew Russell (1992). He writes that "even when cultural borrowing had taken place, in the process of transition cultural elements were often changed subtly, either knowingly or unconsciously, as they became part of the loosely bounded field we could label Yakha (*sic*) culture" (1992:96).

This is an important observation, which is relevant to the other Kirata communities as well. In most instances of cultural contact, borrowing is not only selective but also indigenised. Any element which has no relevance for the receiving culture, or which is incompatible to it, is either discarded or moulded in such a way that it becomes acceptable. This is not to undermine the role of the state in homogenising the cultures or undermining the subjugated cultures. But, such homogenising takes place only at the surface level as has happened among the Kirata communities. The moment the state loosens it grip over the subjugated cultures they begin to revitalise what they consider to be their true 'culture'. Reverting to one's own culture may also take place when the state imposes the homogenising process or when the dominant/surrogate community becomes too repressive or discriminatory as in Darjeeling. In certain cases, such revitalisation also takes place due to the perceived benefits of such a process elsewhere.

But the horizontal spread of the Hindu culture in Nepal is probably just what its propagators —the Upadhyaya Bahuns in particular—wanted. A vertical spread may not have threatened their privilege of being the priestly class but would probably decrease their clientele, which was a major consideration for this section of the Bahuns. But since the spread of the Hindu culture was horizontal, the indigenous culture of the Kirata communities could revive to some extent. The chances of the Kirata cultures becoming more marginalised would have been higher if the spread of the Hindu culture had not been coupled with the furtherance of Tagadhari interests in the historically non-Tagadhari cultural milieus. The Kirata communities in east Nepal in particular not only saw the Bahuns and Chhetris as messengers of a great tradition but also the representatives of the state in usurping their communal and private lands through various means, mostly unscrupulous.

The objective differences in culture between the Tagadhari and Kirata categories have been bridged to a large extent in the last couple of centuries. But it is also perhaps wrong, as the mainstream Nepalese scholars have been insisting, to essentialise the cultural interdependence between the two categories and ignore the critical differences. After all, this interface cannot be, and is perhaps never, the same from the point of view of different cultures.

Socio-economic Relations

The socio-economic relations between the two categories are discussed here on the basis of education, occupation and landholding though these three parameters are not exhaustive of the broad spectrum of such relations.

a) Education: The Tagadharis have had an old tradition of informal education, where the reading of scriptures and other sacred texts is learnt at home. This was by no means confined to those who aspired to become priests or astrologers. This tradition may have contributed to their better achievement in the field of formal education as well, as seen in Table XIII.

Table XIII: *Education of Kiratas (K) and Tagadharis (T)* (in %)

Educational categories	*Yangnam*		*Chhinamakhu*		*Madi Mulkharka*		*Total*	
	K	*T*	*K*	*T*	*K*	*T*	*K*	*T*
Infants	14.7	6.5	11.8	9.3	11.5	9.5	12.7	8.4
Illiterate	44.1	25.8	22.6	29.6	39.7	21.5	35.5	25.6
Primary educated	18.1	22.6	26.9	31.5	12.8	39.0	19.3	31.0
Secondary educated	22.5	45.1	30.8	20.3	28.3	26.0	27.1	30.5
College+ educated	0.6	0.0	7.9	9.3	7.7	4.0	5.4	4.4
Total	631	31	279	108	78	200	988	339

Source: Fieldwork, 1992–93

Though the educational position of the Tagadharis is not better than that of the Kiratas in all the three villages at secondary and college-plus levels, their achievement must be appreciated in view of their later migration to this region. Being late migrants, some of them are too poor to send their children to schools and colleges.

b) Occupation: It is difficult to pinpoint the traditional occupations of these two categories. The traditional occupations of the Kiratas included hunting, trading, the military and agriculture. Of these, the last occupation is the most important for both categories though the traditional occupations of the Tagadharis have been priesthood, agriculture, the military, astrology, and the like. Serving in the armed forces was confined to the

Chhetris in the past but it was only one of their occupations. Outside Nepal, the Tagadharis were never favoured by the British for recruitment into their army and the same tradition largely continues till today. Priesthood is still practised but only by a few members of a particular section of this category called the Upadhyaya Bahuns. The other class of Bahuns called the Jaisis were not allowed to be priests. In this context, it is necessary to quote a section of the royal order issued on 23 September 1761 by the king, Prithivinarayan Shah, in the name of the Jaisis of Nepal:

> Henceforth, Upadhyaya Brahmans shall perform six functions, but Jaisis shall perform only three. Jaisis may study, but not teach. They may perform *yajnyas* but not conduct them. They may make ritual gifts (*dana*) but not accept them (*RRC* 2(12)1970:278).

Even today the Jaisis do not practise priesthood, which is an exclusive privilege of the Upadhyaya Bahuns. But excepting this class of Bahuns, no other caste or community has any exclusive traditional right over any particular occupation. Like the Kiratas, the Tagadharis (including the Upadhyaya Bahuns) are today distributed over a wide range of occupations as shown inTable XIV.

Table XIV: ***Occupations of Kiratas (K) and Tagadharis (T) (in %)***

Occupations	*Yangnam*		*Chhinamakhu*		*Madi Mulkharka*		*Total*	
	K	*T*	*K*	*T*	*K*	*T*	*K*	*T*
Infants	14.7	6.5	11.8	9.3	11.5	9.5	12.7	8.4
Students	25.0	45.1	36.1	41.7	24.4	44.5	28.5	43.8
Household workers	5.5	12.9	7.9	1.9	6.4	5.0	6.6	6.6
Agriculturists	50.7	19.4	33.0	38.0	48.7	30.0	44.1	29.1
Service(wo)men	3.5	12.9	10.8	5.4	9.0	6.5	7.8	8.3
Business(wo)men	0.6	0.0	0.4	0.9	0.0	3.5	0.3	1.5
Others*	0.0	3.2	0.0	2.8	0.0	1.0	0.0	2.3
Total	631	31	279	108	78	200	988	339

* Priesthood and weaving
Source: Fieldwork, 1992–93

There are some finer distinctions regarding occupation that exist between the two categories that are not visible in the statistics in the table. For instance, 'service' for the Kiratas means mostly armed services in a foreign country like India, Hongkong, Singapore or Brunei. But for the Tagadharis it means teaching and office jobs. Whenever they are in the armed services they are within their own country, that is, Nepal. Further, 'household work' is mostly the domain of the women in both categories but whereas the Tagadhari women are free during menstruation, from some household chores like cooking and worshipping, the Kirata women are involved in them all the time.

Landholding

Until about two hundred years ago, the Tagadhari population was rather insignificant in east Nepal. It was only after east Nepal came under Gorkha rule in the early 1770s that it increased considerably. Yet, until the abolition of the *kipat* system in the mid-nineteenth century, most of the Tagadharis held the status of *raitis* or tenants with only usufructory rights over the land. There were, of course, some who had acquired ownership rights over land through the favours of their caste brethren in high official posts. But their legal position was not very clear until the abolition of the *kipat* system. This was one of the reasons why the state felt it necessary to formally abolish this system.

Table XV: ***Landholding of Kiratas (K) and Tagadharis (T) (in %)***

Nature of land	*Yangnam*		*Chhinamakhu*		*Madi Mulkharka*		*Total*	
	K	*T*	*K*	*T*	*K*	*T*	*K*	*T*
Irrigated	29.4	41.3	44.1	56.6	32.6	35.2	35.3	44.4
Unirrigated	56.2	58.7	28.1	37.7	7.5	51.4	30.6	49.3
Cardamom	12.6	0.0	7.7	4.6	19.5	13.4	13.3	6.0
Fallow/Waste	1.8	0.0	20.1	1.1	40.4	0.0	20.8	0.3
% of Landholding	94.3	2.8	72.0	18.9	26.0	35.3	64.1	19.0
% of Households	87.3	4.3	60.6	23.5	16.5	42.4	54.8	23.4

Source: Fieldwork, 1992–93

The Kiratas have a limited amount of irrigated and unirrigated land and are mostly left with fallow/wastelands. This is because in some cases they have sold off their prime lands to meet various expenses like marriage, court cases and gambling, and shifted to the periphery of the villages after clearing the forests or reclaiming wasteland.

On the basis of socio-economic parameters, no clear distinction can be found between the two social categories. However, on the whole, the Tagadharis have a better position vis-à-vis the Kiratas, which becomes even better when viewed in the historical context.

Kiratas and Other Mongoloids

The Kirata and Other Mongoloid groups have relatively less clear boundaries than seen above. There are a lot of cultural, racial and even political overlaps between them making it difficult for an outsider to distinguish between their members. Even linguistically, Risley *et al.* (1931/1975:109) consider these two categories as falling in the "Tibeto-Chinese family, Tibeto-Burman Branch, Tibeto-Himalayan sub-branch".

The "Tibeto-Himalayan sub-branch" actually consists of the "pronominalized Himalayan languages" belonging to the Other Mongoloids and "non-pronominalized Himalayan languages" belonging to the Kiratas. Even historically, a distinction can be drawn between these two categories in the context of east Nepal. The Kiratas are 'indigenous' people of east Nepal whereas the Other Mongoloids have migrated to that region from the western and northern parts of Nepal or beyond. The only exception here should perhaps be made of the *kipat*-owning Sunuwars and Hayus, who are 'indigenous' to this part of Nepal. Further, the Kiratas live in the middle hills whereas some of the Other Mongoloid communities like the Tamang, Sherpa and Gurung are traditionally high-altitude dwellers. Linguistically again, each constituent community of the Other Mongoloid category has its own language though only the Newars have a script of their own. Like in all languages, there are dialectical variations in each Other Mongoloid language though this is not equally significant in the case of the Yakkhas.

Cultural Relations

Both the Kirata and Other Mongoloid categories belong to what Robert Redfield (1956) calls 'Little Traditions'. The Kiratas are, however, in many senses a part of the Great Tradition called 'Hindu' whereas the Other Mongoloid groups are a part of the Hindu as well as the Buddhist traditions. But the incorporation of these two categories into Hindu or Buddhist traditions is peripheral. They are therefore better conceived as Little Traditions.

The main justification for this concept is that the various communities included in these two categories are 'animists'. They worship family, clan, village and forest deities depending on the circumstances and as decided by the various forms of divinations by their own sacred priests. They generally do not practise idol worship nor construct a permanent altar or place of worship as in the Great Traditions. They are also characterised by an absence of written texts or scriptures of their own and rely entirely on oral traditions. There are, of course, many among them who use the written texts of Hindus or Buddhists to perform rites and rituals. But these are later adoptions. Blood sacrifice, which is renounced by many Great Traditions, is also a part of their religious practices.

On the similarities between the two categories may be added what Lionel Caplan has described as the "pleasure complex" (1970:67–69). They are a part of the same 'pleasure complex' characterised by drinking, gambling, smoking, dancing and non-vegetarianism. Hence the word 'matwali', which is an Indo-Aryan cultural concept incorporating both the Kiratas and Other Mongoloids. Though this concept, as an instrument of the Hindu discourse, is applied only to the members of these categories, empirical evidence shows that the Tagadharis are not completely free from this 'complex'. This is particularly true of the Chhetris, who occupy a stratum lower than that of the Bahuns in the social hierarchy of the Nepalis. On the other hand, many belonging to the Kirata or Other Mongoloid category have abandoned the 'pleasure complex' under the influence of certain Vaisnavite sects like the Pranami Dharma, Josmani Dharma and Kabir Panthi. Even the neo-Christians have abandoned this complex to a significant extent.

The Aryan theory on 'matwali' has, however, become counter-productive after the resurgence of the culture of politics in the eastern Himalayas. The word 'matwali', instead of being discarded as pejorative, is captalised as a concept for (re)forming solidarity among all the Mongoloid communities, including the Kiratas. Even the Untouchables are finding a space in this movement as they are also 'matwali', though not described so earlier. In other words, 'matwali' has transformed itself from a symbol of inferiority into one of pride for the non-Tagadhari communities.

Drinking is actually a personal habit found among all castes and communities in Nepal as well as Darjeeling and Sikkim. Some drink in private, others do so in public; some drink expensive alcohol, others cannot afford to; some brew liquor at home, others buy it from them. Yet some critical differences can be seen between the Tagadharis and non-Tagadharis. For instance, among the Kirata communities malt or liquor is essential as a gift during marriage and the very negotiation of marriage is not complete without it. Finally, it is the commonest means of expressing respect and hospitality to guests and visitors. It is offered at the time of festivals, and also to the spirit of the deceased. A quarrel is settled with a penalty of alcohol to be paid by the offender.

Further, both the categories pay bride-wealth. The main marriage ceremony takes place at the groom's house and it is his family which bears part of the expenses incurred in the marriage ceremony even at the bride's house. They also have their own priests to conduct the ceremony, which sometimes involves blood sacrifices to augur a happy life for the couple.

Another important characteristic which separates these two categories from the Tagadharis is the concept of *gotra*. There is only one *gotra* (*Lhasa Gotra*) for most Other Mongoloid communities and two (*Lhasa* and *Kanshi*) for the Kirata communities. The Tagadharis, on the other hand, have innumerable *gotra*s, named after each *rishi*, or sage of the Vedic times. More significantly, *gotra*s are exogamous groups for the Tagadharis but not so for the Kiratas and Other Mongoloids. To the Kiratas, for instance, *Kanshi Gotra* simply means that those belonging to it cannot eat beef whereas those belonging to the *Lhasa Gotra* can, without feeling that it is a sin to do so. And both can drink, inter- or intra-marry without any restriction. T. N. Madan has rightly pointed out that "the people themselves mean different things by the term *gotra*, reflecting caste and tribal differences and perhaps, regional differences also" (1962:59).

Finally, the communities constituting the Kirata or Other Mongoloid categories are linguistic minorities in Nepal today (figures are percentages): Newar (3.0), Gurung (1.2), Tamang (3.5), Mangar (1.4), Limbu (0.9), Rai (1.5), Sherpa (0.9), Sunuwar (0.1) and others. (Bandhu 1989:123). They are theoretically bilingual but their languages have suffered so much due to the state's linguistic policy that many Kiratas and most Other Mongoloid communities in east Nepal are unilingual (Nepali) for all practical purposes. The new-found enthusiasm to develop, protect and preserve their respective languages has a lot of promise but no one can guarantee that, as learning is always easier than de-learning. This also becomes difficult when education is associated with job, career, status, power and the like. In these respects, the Nepali language has all the advantages.

Socio-economic Relations

As in the previous section, the socio-economic relations between the Kiratas and Other Mongoloids shall be discussed here on the basis of education, occupation and landholding.

a) Education: Some of the Mongoloid communities like Tamang, Gurung and Sherpa had come under Buddhist influence and were consequently exposed to reading and writing in the monasteries well before formal education began. But since such education was imparted in the Tibetan language and script, it was confined to only a few persons and this tradition had little or no influence on their formal education, as is evident from Table XVI.

Table XVI: ***Education of Kiratas (K) and Other Mongoloids (OM) (in %)***

Educational categories	*Yangnam*		*Chhinamakhu*		*Madi Mulkharka*		*Total*	
	K	*OM*	*K*	*OM*	*K*	*OM*	*K*	*OM*
Infants	14.7	16.7	11.8	14.8	11.5	14.0	12.7	15.2
Illiterates	44.7	16.7	22.6	45.9	39.7	29.4	35.7	30.7
Primary educated	18.1	33.3	26.9	21.3	12.9	38.4	19.3	31.0
Secondary educated	21.9	33.3	30.8	14.8	28.2	16.8	26.9	21.5
College+ educated	0.6	0.0	7.9	3.2	7.7	1.4	5.4	1.5
Total	631	6	279	61	78	143	988	210

Source: Fieldwork, 1992–93

b) Occupation: Occupation-wise, one may expect some differences between these two categories because certain Other Mongoloid communities like the Sherpa and the Gurung, who are high altitude dwellers, have traditionally depended a lot on trade and pastoralism rather than on agriculture as the middle hill dwelling Kiratas have. Some reflection of these peculiarities may be observed in Table XVII.

Table XVII: ***Occupations of Kiratas (K) and Other Mongoloids (OM) (in %)***

Occupations	*Yangnam*		*Chhinamakhu*		*Madi Mulkharka*		*Total*	
	K	*OM*	*K*	*OM*	*K*	*OM*	*K*	*OM*
Infants	14.7	16.7	11.8	14.8	11.5	14.0	12.7	15.2
Students	25.0	49.9	36.1	18.0	24.4	34.2	28.5	34.0
Household workers	5.5	0.0	7.9	18.0	6.4	5.6	6.6	7.9
Agriculturists	50.7	0.0	33.0	37.7	48.7	43.4	44.1	27.0
Service (wo)men	3.5	16.7	10.8	8.1	9.0	2.8	7.8	9.2
Business (wo)men	0.6	16.7	0.4	3.4	0.0	0.0	0.3	6.7
Total	631	6	279	61	78	143	988	210

Source: Fieldwork, 1992–93

The better position of the Other Mongoloid category in service is primarily due to the Newars, who are a well-known business community in Nepal as well as in Darjeeling and Sikkim.

c) Landholding: Like the Tagadharis, the Other Mongoloids are migrants to the three villages under study. Yet they have already found a safe niche in these villages of east Nepal.

Table XVIII: *Landholding of Kiratas (K) and Other Mongoloids (OM) (in %)*

Nature of land	*Yangnam*		*Chhinamakhu*		*Madi Mulkharka*		*Total*	
	K	*OM*	*K*	*OM*	*K*	*OM*	*K*	*OM*
Irrigated	29.4	0.0	44.1	37.1	32.6	30.6	35.4	22.6
Unirrigated	56.2	12.5	28.1	57.3	7.5	61.4	30.6	43.7
Cardamom	12.6	87.5	7.7	2.8	19.5	6.9	13.3	32.4
Fallow/Waste	1.8	0.0	20.1	2.8	40.4	1.1	20.7	1.3
% of Landholding	94.3	0.3	72.0	7.6	26.0	32.3	64.1	13.4
% of Households	87.3	0.8	60.6	13.3	16.7	30.3	54.8	14.8

Source: Fieldwork, 1992–93

This position of the Other Mondoloids vis-à-vis land is slightly better than that of the Tagadharis in these three villages (see Table XV), chiefly perhaps due to the earlier migration of the Other Mongoloids, particularly the Gurungs and Sherpas, to these villages.

On the basis of the three socio-economic parameters no significant difference can be seen between the Kirata and Other Mongoloid categories. Even the cultural differences between them are rather negligible. Hence the Kirata and Other Mongoloid categories may, if the political situation demands it, come together and form a single, viable political force.

Kiratas and Untouchables

The cultural realm of the Untouchables blends with that of the Tagadharis, but the social and mental spaces between these two categories are worlds apart. The socio-economic upliftment of the Untouchables is a constitutional obligation in India, which has made their position relatively better here than in Nepal. The lax caste system, better spread of education, and more liberal values in Darjeeling and Sikkim, have provided a more open social atmosphere for them to live in than that which still exists in Nepal.

According to the *Brahmanda Purana*, the Untouchables included a host of people described as 'animists', Jain, infidel Brahmans, Shaivites and atheists (see Sharma 1982:65). But today, membership to this category is decided by birth. Temporarily, untouchability is found even among the

Tagadharis during certain stages in life like menstruation and mourning but there is a qualitative difference between these two types of untouchability. The former is permanent in the sense that it continues through generations whereas the latter is temporary. The former affects everyone born into such a family whereas the latter affects the females of a certain age group and males under certain circumstances, like mourning. Further, the former is socially incapacitating whereas the latter is socially liberating, at least temporarily in the sense that such polluted persons need not do the many chores that they would normally have to.

Cultural Relations

The Untouchables not only have cultural and linguistic similarities with the Tagadharis but even racially belong to the same group. In this regard, Parasmani Pradhan writes: "Kamis, Damai, Sarki, and Badi seem to be the progeny of Brahmans and Chhetris of Nepal but seem to have been relegated by them for some unsocial behaviour" (1978:283). This is also attested to by the fact that the surnames of these two categories are mostly the same. Like the Tagadharis again, the Untouchable groups have no language other than Nepali.

Further, the principles governing the institution of *gotra* are exactly the same for the Tagadharis and the Untouchables. Not only are the *gotra* names similar but also the marital significance attached. In both the categories, members of a *gotra* believe that they are descendants of a common ancestor who, in either case, happens to be a Vedic saint. There are also similarities in the rites of passage.

Thus, the Untouchables are culturally closer to the Tagadharis than the Kiratas. But their relationship should perhaps be seen not merely in terms of similarities but also in terms of relations of dominance. If we are to conceptualise Nepali society as a vertical pole, the Tagadharis occupy the top and the Untouchables occupy the bottom while the middle layers are occupied by the Kiratas and Other Mongoloids. Despite lesser cultural similarities with the Kiratas, the Tagadharis consider them as *pani chal ne jat* or 'from whom water can be taken' but the Untouchables are considered *pani na chal ne jat*, or 'from whom water cannot be taken'. A Kirata or Other Mongoloid person is simply *ajat* (of a different caste) but an Untouchable is a *kujat* (literally, of foul caste). An Untouchable is not even allowed to sit on the verandah, let alone enter a house. And he, in the past, had to step aside from the road and say '*jadao*' to an approaching Bahun, Chhetri or a member of a touchable caste (for details, see Subba 1989).

Even in Darjeeling and Sikkim there are restrictions on the Kiratas from taking water or food from Untouchables. While they may drink together they normally do not share the same mug or glass. But instances where such restrictions are not maintained have also been reported (Subba 1989:60). Such deviations from the traditional caste strictures have been possible mainly due to class mobility, though rather limited, among the Untouchables. The world for the poor and illiterate among them however has not changed yet, though their educated and rich brethren have been largely successful in breaking the commensal, if not marital, barriers of the society.

The Kiratas are traditionally a non-caste, segmentary people with no concept of purity and pollution or even hierarchy within their own system. But under the influence of the Hindu Tagadharis, for the last couple of centuries they have imbibed many such caste traits, which they find difficult to abandon today. Some of them have stopped worshipping certain Hindu deities like Ram, Vishnu and Krishna or celebrating festivals like *Dashain* and *Tihar* but they live very much within the caste discourse. Their anti-Hindu stance is therefore shaky and liable to be liquidated at any point of time unless they can reinvent and strongly invigorate their own traditions. The signs of such an effort have already begun to appear in the naming of their children and popularising of certain traditional Kirata dance-forms and festivals (see Chapter 7). Earlier, the naming of children was a privilege of the Brahman priests though the parents did not strictly call their children by their horoscope names. But the practice of every child having a horoscope prepared by a Brahman and consulting it prior to long-distance travel or marriage was received from the Tagadharis and this was to a large extent responsible for detribalising the Kiratas and Other Mongoloids in Nepal as well as outside it. This may also be cited as an instance of the Hindu discourse decentering non-Hindu cosmology.

Socio-economic Relations

The Untouchables in Nepal, far from being protected by the state through various legislations, have been historically subjected to different forms of exploitation, humiliation and subjugation. Their socio-economic status is thus, as expected, quite poor vis-a-vis other categories in Nepal.

a) Education: It should be remembered here that the Untouchables rarely have any commensal and marital interaction with the Kiratas or other categories. But there is no restriction on their attending schools along with the members of other categories. Thus, if they are educationally backwarc it is due not so much to their caste status as it is, perhaps, to their economic or familial handicaps.

Table XIX: ***Education of Kiratas (K) and Untouchables (U) (in %)***

Educational categories	*Yangnam*		*Chhinamakhu*		*Madi Mulkharka*		*Total*	
	K	*U*	*K*	*U*	*K*	*U*	*K*	*U*
Infants	14.7	23.6	11.8	8.3	11.5	11.8	12.7	14.6
Illiterates	44.7	52.7	22.8	41.7	39.7	49.0	35.7	47.8
Primary educated	18.1	14.5	26.9	25.0	12.8	27.5	19.3	22.3
Secondary educated	21.7	9.2	30.6	25.0	28.2	11.7	26.8	15.3
College+ educated	0.8	0.0	7.9	0.0	7.8	0.0	5.5	0.0
Total	631	55	279	12	78	51	988	118

Source: Fieldwork, 1992–93

b) Occupation: Traditionally the Kami, Sarki and Damai have beer ironsmiths, cobblers and tailors or musicians. But it is difficult to accep that these were their only occupations: agriculture must have been a majo: source of income even in the past, though it is probable that they were agricultural labourers or tenants more than owner-cultivators. Their traditional occupations must have been whole-time engagements only for those who were on the pay roll of the Gorkha rulers. Even today, the situatior is the same, except in the urban areas where the cobblers and tailors finc a larger clientele to engage them full time.

Table XX: ***Occupations of Kiratas (K) and Untouchables (U) (in %)***

Occupations	*Yangnam*		*Chhinamakhu*		*Madi Mulkharka*		*Total*	
	K	*U*	*K*	*U*	*K*	*U*	*K*	*U*
Infants	14.7	23.6	11.8	8.3	11.5	11.8	12.7	14.6
Students	25.0	14.5	36.2	16.7	24.4	23.5	28.5	18.2
Household workers	5.5	5.5	7.8	0.0	6.4	15.7	6.6	7.1
Agriculturists	50.4	40.0	33.0	16.7	48.7	39.2	44.0	31.9
Service (wo)men	3.8	5.5	10.8	0.0	9.0	2.0	7.9	2.5
Business (wo)men	0.6	3.6	0.4	0.0	0.0	0.0	0.3	1.2
Others*	0.0	7.3	0.0	58.3	0.0	7.8	0.0	24.5
Total	631	55	279	12	78	51	988	118

* Tailoring, ironsmithy and weaving

Source: Fieldwork, 1992–93.

c) Landholding: The position of the Untouchables vis-à-vis landholding is not better than that of the Kiratas for various historical, social and other reasons.

Table XXI: *Landholding of Kiratas (K) and Untouchables (U) (in %)*

Nature of land	Yangnam		Chhinamakhu		Madi Mulkharka		Total	
	K	U	K	U	K	U	K	U
Irrigated	29.4	10.1	44.1	44.4	32.6	61.9	35.4	38.8
Unirrigated	56.2	89.9	28.1	55.6	7.5	26.5	30.6	57.3
Cardamom	12.6	0.0	7.7	0.0	19.5	10.7	13.3	3.6
Fallow/Waste	1.8	0.0	20.1	0.0	40.4	0.9	20.7	0.3
% of Landholding	94.3	2.6	72.0	1.4	26.0	6.4	64.1	3.5
% of Households	87.3	7.6	60.6	2.6	16.5	10.8	54.8	7.0

Source: Fieldwork, 1992–93

The relationship between the Kiratas and other categories varies from village to village depending on their history, demographic composition and the socio-economic criteria. On the whole, it is observed that cultural differences are more significant than socio-economic differences. To be more specific, the Kiratas seem to have closer cultural linkages with Other Mongoloids than with the Tagadharis and Untouchables. The perception of such cultural difference is, however, influenced not only by centuries of Tagadhari rule in Nepal but also by Hindu discourse which has influenced all the categories. The contribution of western anthropologists to the widening of this gap, if any, is perhaps insignificant in comparison to the much stronger historical, political and discursive influences operating otherwise.

In any situation of interface, it is the perception of respective cultures which is perhaps more significant than the empirical situations. And this perception can be cultivated by motivated persons who may present their own version of the ground realities. More often than not, perceptions differ at the level of culture and no matter how hard the state or its surrogate community tries, they often fail to overlap. The present situation in Nepal is a case in point. It may be further aggravated by the Kiratas' perception of an 'imagined' situation, which was better than that which exists today.

7

Foundations of Kirata Nationalism

The objective of this chapter is to explore the foundations of Kirata nationalism, which is an exercise some of the Kirata scholars and leaders themselves are actively engaged in. This basically involves two things: one, (re)creating the Kirata nation, which means picking up certain commonalities and ignoring the differences within the groups categorised here as 'Kirata'; and two, showing how such features differ from those existing among other categories, particularly the Tagadharis. This is not an easy task, nor one that can be concluded here, but an ongoing process.

Culture, language and religion among the Kiratas vis-à-vis other categories are discussed here as the foundations of Kirata nationalism. Culture, as it is generally understood, encompasses language and religion too, but for the purpose of the present book they are discussed separately. Even intermarriage among the Kirata groups is considered to be an important foundation of their nationalism but this aspect has not been dealt with here.

Culture

Before discussing Kirata culture it is necessary to bear in mind that the kiratas have been variously influenced by the Hindus from the west Buddhists from the north and east, and, over the last hundred years or so Christians from the south. The most important and all-pervading is obviously that of the Hindus, not only in Nepal but also in Darjeeling and Sikkim. Some aspects have been so completely internalised that it is indeed difficult to separate them from what the Kiratas consider as their 'traditional', pre-Hindu or pre-Buddhist, culture. In certain cases, such efforts are even resisted from within, and the entire exercise tends to become counter-productive to the formation of their nationalism. Hence, too much emphasis on their 'ideal' culture is not only dangerous but also unrealistic. Even the testimony of *mundhum* is not easily accepted by all because it can have multiple interpretations.

The Limbus, Yakkhas and those Rais who are settled in Limbuan since ancient times have almost the same rites of passage regarding the days, months or years when a rite is to be observed, the nature of the rite itself, and its social implications. The Rai rites of passage, on the other hand, vary in certain respects within themselves (see Toba 1992 for details). The internal variation among Rais can be attributed primarily to the Buddhist influences in the northern and Hindu influences in the middle hills of Nepal. However, such differences are essentially a matter of detail and need not always be taken seriously.

The Kirata birth rites are basically three: the naming, the rice-feeding and the hair-cutting ceremonies of which the last is performed only for the male child. The first ceremony takes place on the fourth day for a boy and third day for a girl amongst the Limbus and Yakkhas, and sixth and fifth days respectively amongst the Rais. In fact, the Limbus have one pre-birth ceremony called *sapok-chomen* which, according to Songpangphe (1992:3), takes place during the sixth month after conception and, according to Aasman Subba (1988:28), during the ninth month after conception. However, in Yangnam, it was reported that it could be held on any day before the delivery of the child as it is essentially meant for propitiating the deities so that miscarriages and foetal or infantile deaths are averted. Such a rite is not reported from among the other two Kirata groups, which indicates that foetal or infantile deaths were perhaps more frequent among the Limbus.

The naming ceremony is very similar among the groups, despite the variation in the number of days between the Limbus/Yakkhas and the Rais. The house has to be purified in the morning by daubing it with a mixture of clay and cowdung and by burning the incense of dry pine leaves. The priest (*phedangma* or *mangpa* as the case may be), relatives and neighbours are usually invited, and food and drinks are offered to them. Before the rite, the ceremonial bathing of the mother and the child with warm water is essential. And the rite invariably includes the recitation of the *mundhum* (or *muddum*) by the priest, and seeking the approval and blessings of the household and clan deities. The language used by the priests depends, interestingly, not on his own language, but on the language of his patron-deity.

This ceremony, called *nwaran*, takes place on the eleventh day in the case of the Tagadharis. The naming ceremony among them depends on the exact time of birth and the position of the stars. The day on which this ceremony is to take place is therefore decided by an astrologer. However, the cleansing of the 'impure' mother and child and the daubing of the house is essential. Inviting relatives and neighbours to a feast is also common.

The next important birth ceremony of the Kiratas is the rice-feeding ceremony. This takes place during the fourth month for a boy and third month for a girl among the Limbus/Yakkhas and on the sixth and fifth months respectively among the Rais. As in the naming ceremony, the ceremonial cleansing of the mother, the child and the house is a prerequisite. The presence of the child's relatives, both paternal and maternal, a priest and the neighbours are also ensured on this occasion. The manner in which the child is fed varies across the three Kirata communities and across the three villages studied, but the child is essentially given some water, cereals and juice. Further, the priests officiating on such occasions pray to the supernatural powers to ensure the child a healthy and long life. This occasion is also concluded with a feast.

This ceremony is called *pasni* among the Tagadharis. It normally takes place during the seventh month for a boy and fifth for a girl. As with the other ceremonies, for this too, the house and child are cleansed, food of various kinds is prepared, and the maternal and paternal relatives of the child besides other villagers are invited.

The final birth ceremony of the Kiratas is the hair-cutting ceremony, which normally takes place when the child is three. The cutting of hair is preferably done by a maternal uncle though even a classificatory uncle can do it. In this ceremony also, the daubing of the house, the inviting of relatives and neighbours to a feast, and the presence of a priest are considered essential among all the Kirata communities. The point of significance here is the practice of hair shaving among the Rais of the middle hills. This is considered to be a mark of Hindu influence.

This ceremony, called *chuda-karma*, takes place when the child is five or seven among the Tagadharis. This is to be done by the boy's maternal uncle though, again, a classificatory maternal uncle can officiate. Once the head is shaven, it is important to retain a tuft of hair at the back as a sign of being a Hindu. This is followed by all those Rais who practise hair shaving wherever they are.

With the hair-cutting ceremony end the birth rites of the Kirata boys and there is no ritual till marriage, whereas, for a girl they end with the rice-feeding ceremony itself. But not so among the Tagadharis. For a Tagadhari boy, there is another important ceremony called *bratabanda* or sacred thread ceremony which takes place when he is seven or nine years old if a Bahun and thirteen or fifteen years if a Chhetri boy. A Tagadhari girl has to undergo a confinement for a fortnight when she attains her menarche. She cannot see nor can she be seen by her male siblings or relatives then. She has to undergo similar confinement for seven days during her second menstruation and then for four days on subsequent occasions. But she can see and be seen by her brothers on all such occasions except the first (Bista 1980:14–15). This indicates the fear of incest since early times.

The Kiratas do not have such rituals based on the concept of pollution nor are they particularly strict about the rites described earlier. The presence of the priest, for instance, is more common among the Kiratas of Nepal than those of Darjeeling and Sikkim. In the latter areas, such traditional priests have become so rare that they are not easily available for every occasion. The Limbus of Tanek village, Kalimpong, now go to Sikkim whenever they need a *phedangma* after the one in the village died. It is perhaps due to such problems that a concession has been made that any elderly man who has some idea about such work may officiate as priest.

As regards the apparent gender bias among the Kiratas marked by the differential days, months or years for boys and girls, the difference is clearly more symbolic than real. In terms of the extravaganza or excitement it is always more in the case of the first child, whether son or daughter. The birth of a daughter does not necessarily bring any unhappiness among them as it does among many dowry-giving societies. This is because of the fact that the Kiratas are bride-wealth receiving societies. The married daughters are given some copper/brass utensils, a heifer, and some clothes and ornaments depending on the economic condition of their natal families but these are not considered as dowry.

Coming to marriage, there are more deviations here from the ideal practices than the birth rites. Marriage rituals depend primarily on whether or not a marriage is formal or informal, negotiated or decided through other socially approved (or not) means. It may be further noted that the ideal rituals of a marriage are the same among all the three Kirata communities: what varies is the degree of Hinduisation and its impact on their traditional marriage practices.

A negotiated or formal Kirata marriage essentially includes four stages which are called *char kalam*. The first stage involves going to the girl's house with a group of relatives led by a go-between and seeking her consent. The leader, called *kalhiya*, may be any elderly person who knows the art of speaking in flowery language. He may not belong to the boy's clan but he has to be a member of the community. He occupies the centre-stage and the ritual credit for having arranged the marriage goes to him. But before this, the sisters, aunts and sisters-in-law of the boy would have laid the foundation for such a negotiation. Though they are never given any credit socially, they have to face a lot of criticism if the boy or girl does not live up to the expectation of his or her family members and relatives.

The second event is bringing the bride home; the third includes the blessing of the couple by their senior (in age and relationship) relatives and what is called *saino kelaunu* or literally 'exchanging of kinship terms' between the parents and older relatives of the couple. In this ritual, one senior relative introduces the girl to the boy's relatives and the boy to the girl's relatives. In both cases, the couple has to touch the feet of such relatives and seek their blessing. The fourth and final stage is marked by bringing the bride home with gifts of food, malt, alcohol and even money for her parents and relatives. Each stage is, in fact, a complex of elaborate activities which are governed by the principles of their *mundhum*. Even those non-negotiated or elopement marriages (but which do not violate the rules of consanguinity) have to pass through the latter two stages of marriage. The only marriages which do not have to pass through any of the four ritual stages are *jari biha* (or marrying somebody else's wife) and *kujat biha* (or marriage with an untouchable).

On the Kulunge Rai marriage, McDougal writes that it is "better described as a process than as an event; there is an interval of several years between the initial and final rites of the union" (1973:215). This is, however, not true of all Rais. For instance, in Chhinamakhu, the entire process does not take more than a year unless the final rite needed to be inadvertently postponed due to the death of a family member or close relative of the bride or groom. Normally, the rearing of pigs and goats for the marriage feast begins a year or more before the parents decide to get their sons married, and the brewing of malt begins about a couple of months before the final rite is fixed; this usually occurs in the winter after harvesting is over. For several reasons no prior arrangement is made for a girl's marriage. Her marriage is a minor event and her parents are often taken unawares by her sudden elopement or a *kalhiya* appearing suddenly one evening to ask for her hand.

There are two important studies by Barnouw (1955) and Allen (1987) on Rai marriages in eastern Nepal. Barnouw makes special mention of *sagun* and *lagan*. The first is a welcoming ceremony for the bride in which a "chicken is killed and some of its blood placed on three plantain leaves, which are set down just inside the door. The girl must step over the blood-smeared leaves when she crosses the threshold" (1955:19). The latter is the climax at which "the boy's parents give their official recognition to the marriage by placing a rice *tika* (forehead mark) on the brow of both boy and girl as they pronounce their blessings" (1955:20). In Chhinamakhu, *lagan* is observed in much the same way as Barnouw describes it, but *sagun* does not involve any blood sacrifice, which could be an influence of Tagadhari culture. However, the couple has to ritually sip millet beer while others shower flowers and coloured rice grains called *achheta* on them as a symbol of blessing.

Allen's work, on the other hand, is an analytical study of the Thulung Rai marriage rituals. Despite his awareness of the conceptual difficulties involved in separately categorising Hindu and tribal marital practices, he says that considerable changes have occurred in the tribal marriage due to Hinduisation (1987:15–33). His observations are, however, not representative of the northern Rais and, to some extent, of the middle hill dwelling Limbus and Yakkhas too, who have largely remained outside Hindu influence. But it is close to most of the three Kirata communities in Darjeeling and Sikkim.

In this regard, the *kelang* or drum dance, which was a concomitant feature of a Limbu or Yakkha marriage earlier, has become rare in Nepal and even rarer in Darjeeling and Sikkim. It is only very recently that this dance form is being revived by them. However, there are certain practical problems that have arisen now such as nonavailability of huge sized *castonopsis* tree trunks for making the drums and of people who know how to dance *kelang* or sing for it. Thus unless some adaptation is made, the new-found enthusiasm may soon be frittered away.

One of the features of Tagadhari marriages absent among the Kiratas is the practice of marrying off girls early, preferably before they reach the age of puberty. This practice is associated with the concept of *punya* or virtue, which they hope to earn by doing so. Though such a practice is gradually being eroded among the Tagadharis due to the spread of education, their daughters get married relatively earlier than those of the Kiratas.

A corollary of this practice, and traditionally considered to be the most important aspect of the Tagadhari marriage, is called *kanyadan* or 'gift of the virgin' to the groom by the bride's parents. This must take place at the exact hour stipulated by an astrologer. The parents must fast for about twenty-four hours before they perform this pious rite. This rite is also uncommon among the Kiratas of the eastern Himalayas.

Some Rai women, on getting married, put vermilion on their forehead in Darjeeling and Sikkim but most of them do not do so in Nepal except, at times, when they go to towns or markets. The necklace of tiny green beads called *potey* is proof enough of their being married. The Tagadhari women also wear this necklace but, unless widowed, they invariably put vermilion on their foreheads.

The most important feature of the Tagadhari marriage, which is distinctly different from the practice of the Kiratas, is that the main marriage ceremony takes place in the house of the bride whereas it takes place in the groom's house among the Kiratas. Even the practice of giving dowry to the groom is reported to have seeped in among the Tagadharis who have come into close contact with the dowry-giving plains people. The reading from the sacred scriptures by the priest who guides the couple and others in this rite is another important symbol of difference from the Kirata marriage. The Kirata marriage is marked by the absence of the Brahman priest and his sacred scriptures, nor is it essential for a *phedangma*, *mangpa* or *nakchhong* to recite the *mundhum*.

Finally, about death rites. Of all the rites of passage, the death rites are perhaps most earnestly performed by the Kiratas and Tagadharis alike. Such rites are taken seriously not just because they do not want to be haunted by the wayward souls of the dead but also because they wish that the souls of such persons find their rightful places in heaven.

On the traditional Limbu death rites, the early British accounts are not very consistent. For instance, Campbell writes:

> They burn the dead, selecting the summits of mountains for the purpose, and afterwards collect and bury the ashes, over which they raise a square tomb of stone, about four feet high, placing an upright stone on its summit. The Limbus do not make offerings, or sacrifices for the dead, nor have they any belief in the transmigration of souls. They mourn the dead by weeping and lamentations at the time, and by avoiding merrymakings, and adorning of hair with flowers for a month or two (1845:79).

It is true that they do not make sacrifices for the dead but offerings are invariably made on such occasions. Dalton reiterates Campbell's view on the Limbu death rituals (1872:103). However, their observations are apparently based on the more Hinduised Limbus than those who still adhere to traditional practices. The usual practice of the disposal of the dead is by burial, not by cremation. Hence the contention of Vansittart (1915:111) is more accurate. John Morris also considers burial to be the Limbu way of disposing of the dead and the recent practice of cremation as a possible influence of "the gradual spread of orthodox Hindu ideas" (1933/1985:92).

Similarly, the Rais practise both burial and cremation. However, Risley writes that the practice of disposing of the dead varies considerably among them. Besides burial or cremation, they are also reported to throw the body into a river or stream (Risley cited in Vansittart 1915:126).

Native literature on death rites shows that the people depend to a large extent on the nature of death, which is broadly classified into natural and unnatural or due to accident, which includes suicidal deaths. But in any case, mourning by not consuming salt, oil and meat continues for four days in the case of a male and three days in the case of a female. However, no mourning takes place in the case of the death of an infant nor does any ritual follow it.

Normally, when an adult dies, his or her eyes are shut, legs and hands straightened, and the body (barring the head) is covered with a clean piece of cloth. When the body is taken to the burial place or crematorium, it is invariably wrapped in a piece of white cloth. The body may be buried or cremated immediately or after a couple of days if they have to wait for the family members living far away to arrive. In the latter case, the body is constantly guarded so that no animal or non-Kirata touches it. This is due to the belief that the soul of the dead person will turn into whatever touches it. The body is carried with the help of a make-shift stretcher made of green bamboo and tied at three places.

The purification ceremony takes place on the fourth day for a man and third day for a woman. On this occasion, the presence of a *phedangma* or *nakchhong* is essential. On that day, the villagers and all the relatives of the dead assemble, particularly those who had joined the funeral procession. A bottle of liquor or strained malt, fried garlic, onion, dry chilly, pieces of ginger and pork are placed on a bamboo winnow. If the deceased was a smoker, tobacco is also laid on it. Then the priest, after completing his recitation from the *mundhum*, announces where and when the person died and specifies the restrictions as well as how long they have to be observed. Next, he addresses the people gathered and requests them to allow the mourners to be free from such restrictions. When permission is granted, the articles laid on the winnow are distributed to the mourners and food is offered to all those who have gathered.

Meanwhile, the head and eyebrows of the junior male relatives of the dead would have been shaven. This has been a subject of much debate among the Limbus today and many of them consider it to be of Aryan import and hence argue that it should be discontinued. The Aryan origin

8

is quite probable in view of the fact that the head is not fully shaved but a tuft of hair at the back is retained, besides being covered with a white cap as done by the Tagadharis. Those who argue against this practice refer to *mundhum* and say that the traditional Limbu practice was not to shave but to leave the hair uncut for an entire year. However, as it stands now, shaving is the rule even among the Limbus and Yakkhas, who are considered to be relatively less influenced by Hinduism than the Rais.

On the evening of the day of purification, a priest conducts an elaborate rite called *tangsing* by the Limbus and Yakkhas. It continues throughout the night. Earlier it was held for three consecutive nights. But now, it is said that, it cannot be practised due to the nonavailability of an accomplished *phedangma*. Ordinary *phedangmas* cannot do it. In this rite, the soul of the dead is called by the priest who then asks it about its unfulfilled desires or reasons for its death in case of unnatural circumstances. The dialogue between the soul and the priest sometimes continues for over an hour and is witnessed by all those elderly persons who can understand the vernacular language used by the priest then. The priest is in a state of trance, shaking vigorously and speaking in the language and voice of the dead. The elderly people gathered there also to persuade the soul of the dead person in different ways so that it agrees to leave the earth and go to heaven. Often, the priest finds it difficult to persuade the soul to leave the earth and it takes a lot of time and several promises before it finally agrees to do so.

Such a rite normally involves the sacrifice of fowls and offering of food, drinks, and tobacco—if the deceased was a smoker. The blood sacrifice is not supposed to take place if the deceased belonged to the *Kanshi Gotra* but in practice it depends on the dictates of the priest. This is also an occasion on which the villagers gather at night, play cards or carrom, and also witness the dramatic performance of the priest.

This concludes the death ceremonies and there is no more rite, annual or occasional, to be performed after that, unlike in the case of the Tagadharis. The Tagadhari death rituals are different in some other respects too. For instance, they mourn the death of senior relatives for thirteen days and such mourning is not only marked by abstinence from salt, oil, meat and merry-making but also by bathing several times a day in cold water and fasting, practices which are not found among the Kiratas. The Tagadharis also abstain, during such a period, from taking food from any person or offering any to others. Further, the male mourners wear a loin cloth. The Kiratas, however, do not have such restrictions.

Most importantly, such Tagadhari mourners have to perform a ritual daily for a couple of hours under the guidance of a Brahman priest. After the conclusion of the mourning period, called *kriya*, a feast is given to all the relatives and villagers and gifts of food, cloth, furniture, utensils, and so on are made to the officiating priest. Besides, they observe the death anniversary called *shraddha*. In this rite, male descendants of the deceased bathe, fast and shave their heads. A ritual is performed by the priest and a small feast is also offered to relatives and neighbours (For details, see Bista 1980:13).

Thus, with regard to the three rites of passage, one notices certain differences between the Kiratas and the Tagadharis. Such differences are particularly important nowadays because their symbolic meanings have assumed political meanings as well.

Language

Early European knowledge about Kirata languages was apparently marred by incomplete information. For instance, Campbell wrote that the Limbu language has no written character and no similarity with the languages of the Lepchas, Bhutias, Meches and Hayus and no connection whatsoever with the Nepali language (1845:80).

About three decades later, Edward Dalton reiterated this when he wrote that "[t]hey have no written character of their own" (1872:103). But they not only had a written character but later studies such as that by Keith Sprigg showed that their script had close affinities with the Tibetan and Lepcha scripts besides being influenced by the Devanagari script at a later stage of its development (see IOL MSS Eur D 537). This script has its origin, according to Balkrishna Pokhrel, a noted linguist, in the Brahmi script (see Kainla 1992:16). It was hardly known until a Limbu scholar called Sirijanga revived it around 1741 in Sikkim. But it could not flourish due to state oppression there as well as in Nepal and it began to be read and taught only after 1925 when Iman Singh Chemjong and a few others gave it a new lease of life in the open atmosphere of Darjeeling (Manen 1984:61–62). At present, this script and language are taught in Sikkim and the language has been recognised as one of the four state languages there, the other three being Nepali, Lepcha and Bhutia.

The *Concise Limbu Grammar and Dictionary* by A. Weidert and B. Subba (1985:1), considers the Limbu language to be the "most important language of the Kiranti group of Tibeto-Burman languages". According to the authors, its linguistic structure is different from other

Kirata languages in many respects. An example of this is the existence of the glottal stop (') in the Limbu language, which is almost absent in the Rai languages. Morphologically too, the Limbu language alone is known to have a fully developed noun declension system. Similarly, the verb system of the Limbu language is "the most fully developed of all Kiranti languages" (1985:2–3).

It appears that there is a great deal of structural homogeneity within the Kirata languages though, as Weidert and Subba argue, the Limbu language may be structurally most developed of all. However, dialectical variations across districts and regions are definitely more pronounced among the Rais than among the Limbus and Yakkhas. Charles McDougal rightly points out that the "degree of local and linguistic differentiation exhibited by the Rais is unique among the tribal, Tibeto-Burman speaking populations of Nepal" (1973:205). And this is well illustrated by Gerd Hanpon in his *Rais of Eastern Nepal: Ethnic and Linguistic Grouping* (1991).

Despite the best efforts of some scholars in trying to trace the morphological similarities among the Kirata languages and similar efforts of various other Kirata organisations dominated by the Limbus, the emergence of a Kirata language seems a distant reality. Hence, language cannot perhaps be a strong foundation of Kirata nationalism though the role of language in nationalism has been much emphasised by Max Boehm (1933). This can be, and is, a strong foundation of Limbu or Yakkha nationalism but not quite so in the case of the Rais. The failure of the Jhapa conference, referred to in the next chapter, to evolve a consensus on the language issue of the Rais is a clear indication of this.

Interestingly, and perhaps rather contradictorily, it is only after the Kiratas became bilinguals, with the Nepali language binding every one of them and the Devanagari script as the common script, does Kirata nationalism seem to have taken root. Thus, it is only in the Nepali language and Devanagari script that communication across the various Kirata groups is possible at present and there is a very slim chance of the Kirata language and script replacing them in the near future. The Rais indicate no wish to accept the Sirijanga script as the Kirata script and some Limbus have now begun to call it their own and not the Kirata script as they did before. But if the ego differences between the Rais and Limbus could be resolved, the Sirijanga script is believed to possess all the phonetic and morphological properties necessary to serve as the Kirata script.

Though the question of script may thus be resolved, the question of language is not expected to be settled as easily. Imposing one language or dialect over others has always been found to be counter-productive to the spirit of nationalism whether it is at the level of nations or nation-states. What binds all the Kirata groups together, therefore, is not the language but a common sense of having lost their respective languages in the wake of the spread of the Nepali language with or without state patronage. For instance, in Nepal, Nepali language speakers increased from 47.0 percent in 1942 to 58.4 percent in 1981 whereas the Limbu and Rai speakers decreased from 1.7 and 2.9 percent to 0.9 and 1.5 percent respectively (Magar 1992). This is considered to be the consequence of the official policy in Nepal which advocates "one race, one religion, one language and one dress". State oppression on the other languages of Nepal did not change even after the bloody revolution of 1950 and remains much the same even after the ushering in of democracy in 1990. It is only recently that some languages like Newari and Rai have been 'permitted' to be taught upto Class V.

The scenario outside Nepal was, however, slightly different. The Sikkim situation prior to 1975 was similar to that of Nepal in many respects but the Nepali language did not receive direct state patronage there as it did in Nepal. Besides, in 1980, even the Limbu language was given official recognition as a state language. In Darjeeling, on the other hand, the situation was such that even the Nepali language had to struggle for a long time to be recognised as an official language in the hill areas of West Bengal. This, however, was possible only with the concerted efforts of all Nepali speakers irrespective of their linguistic backgrounds (see Subba 1992 for details).

In the entire region, the Kirata languages, as also the Other Mongoloid languages, are facing the threat of extinction. This is however not only attributable to state oppression over a long period of time but also to the lack of national consciousness among the speakers of the respective languages. The recent upsurge of nationalism among them holds out a lot of hope and promise for such subjugated languages.

The question of language vis-à-vis nationalism in the Kirata context should perhaps be appreciated in the above sense rather than as a symbol of Kirata nationalism. If the Kiratas decide on homogenising their languages with mass consensus, which seems difficult at this stage or even later, it can emerge as a Kirata symbol.

Religion

Of all the aspects of Kirata nationalism, the most difficult to sort cut is perhaps their religion. The difficulty, however, arises not so much from the range of their religious beliefs and practices as it does from the nomenclature of their religion. Very strenuous efforts have been made to separate their religion from Hinduism or Buddhism, though neither of these has any clearly defined boundaries with what is now called the Kirat Dharma. The word 'animism' would perhaps be the most suitable but this word is known only to a few English-speaking Kiratas and there is a growing consciousness over its pejorative connotation the world over.

Campbell devotes about three pages to the Limbu religion which, according to him, is neither Hindu nor Buddhist but at the same time admits that it is very difficult to "give a name to the one they practise" (1845:76–77). Apart from the names of the gods (most of which are spelt incorrectly by him) the rest of the account is indeed a very close representation of their religion. Edward Dalton also agrees with what Campbell has said and adds that they have "obstinately adhered to their primitive paganism" (1872:102).

Risley discusses the Limbu religion in some detail. He particularly notes their "nonchalant attitude" towards religion (1891/1981:17). He further writes that "the leading principle of the Limbu religion is *animism*" (1891/1981:18, emphasis in original). He argues at length why the word "shamanism" is ill-suited to represent their religion. He writes that the "original religion of the Limbus is closely akin to the Pon or ancient religion of Tibet" (1891/1981:19). This is also confirmed by Allen (1976).

According to Vansittart, the Rais do not have a different system of beliefs and practices from that of the Limbus. He writes that the Rai version of Hinduism was quite lax: they neither adopted Hinduism in full nor did they reject it completely. Even the Buddhistic features found among them were rather crude (1915:102). But Morris says that "both Limbus and Rais do nowadays recognise, even if not very enthusiastically, the Brahman supremacy" (1933:101). He mentions their employing Brahmin priests for naming the children and determining the auspicious date for marriage, but their own traditional priests performed religious and domestic ceremonies (1933:101).

The Kiratas seem to have suffered from a crisis of religious identity for a fairly long period of time. This crisis seems to be due not only to nomenclative indeterminancy but also to the scorn and humiliation by the Tagadharis, who consider themselves superior to the Kiratas. On the other hand, the Kiratas are not only described as 'Hindus' by the official media but actually brought under the Hindu fold through various mechanisms, the most important being the caste system and prohibition of cow slaughter. Those who could not resist such influences (such as the Rais of the middle hills) began to identify themselves with the Hindus and even justify the view that the Kirata religion is a Hindu one based on the Vedas. This has been heightened by the recent enthusiasm of some Limbus to build permanent temples such as in Gangtok and the Panchthar district of Nepal. This shows a certain tension emanating from the desire to live at par with the organised, institutionalised religions. But building temples, even with a Kirata flavour, is unknown in their religious traditions and is perhaps uncalled for.

Some of the Rai intellectuals who have made tremendous efforts to prove the Vedic origin of the Kirata religion are Swami Prapannacharya in his *Vedma ke Chha* (1981) and Gambhir Rai Arya (1980). They have gone to great lengths to show that even their dialects, particularly Chamling and Bantawa, are derived from Sanskrit and the Kiratas are not Mongoloids but Aryans. Though their arguments are overstretched and unconvincing, their efforts may be appreciated in view of the strain which they are under due to the crisis of their religious identity.

Let us now turn to the empirical situation in the Kirata villages. At the outset it may be mentioned that the people worship a host of deities at different periods of time in different ways and for different purposes. These deities are named and may be broadly classified as consanguinal and affinal.[1] Such a classification is normally not made by the non-Kiratas but they too, including the Tagadharis, worship a number of deities who are not included in their scriptures or religious order, in a formal manner.

In Yangnam, all Limbus worship the following three important deities: *Theba Samang* (literally, grandfather god), *Yuma Samang* (or grandmother god), and *Him Samang* (or household god). But besides these three, they also worship a host of other deities which are believed to have been brought by their married women.[2]

There are significant local and clan variations in the manner these deities are worshipped. But for *Theba Samang* only male animals and birds (whether pig, buffalo, fowl or goat) and for *Yuma Samang* only female animals or birds are sacrificed. The worshipping of the three principal deities may be undertaken every year or once in three years but normally it takes place in December, after the harvest. The ritual may be performed inside the house or outside it, though the affinal deities are normally worshipped outside. It is believed that, if not propitiated, they can cause various problems such as backache, 'losing of the soul', and so on.

Chokhoba is worshipped on the day of *Vijayadashami* (usually in October) with the help of a *phedangma*. The colour of the cock to be sacrificed for this deity may be red or white but it must be sacrificed outside the house so that the sun can watch and be pleased. This deity, if angry is believed to cause madness and diarrhoea. *Saba Samang* may be worshipped in the top storey of the house outside it or in the field where a small hut standing on four tall bamboo stilts is constructed to house this deity. The deity is offered fruits, eggs, a cock and milk, and is considered to be an important deity which can, it is said, cause pain in the back or knee, blindness and even an abortion, if neglected.

Most of these deities are worshipped during two periods: *Udhauli* (literally meaning the process of going downwards, towards the south, or when the season changes from hot to cold) and *Ubhauli* (the antonym of *Udhauli*, when the birds and animals start moving northwards, towards higher altitudes). They all need to be propitiated with sacrifices of blood in order to avoid being subjected to different kinds of sicknesses. Each clan is associated with one or two such deities besides the three pan-Limbu deities—*Theba*, *Yuma*, and *Him Samang*.

The Tagadharis do not worship such deities but the Other Mongoloids do. For instance, the Newars worship *Bhimsen* or the household god and the wind god; the Rais worship *Khoklihangma* or the forest goddess, *Samkha* or the hearth god, *Lelemma* or the snake god and *Wairing* or the hunter's god. In all such worship, blood sacrifice is essential in order to please the deities and avoid falling prey to their anger. Similarly, the Untouchables worship various deities called *Kalanki* and *Maharani* besides the Limbu deities like *Yuma* and *Thungdangba*.

There is also a widespread belief in taboo among all castes and communities. The taboos for the Tagadharis such as not eating beef or pork is, however, a question of purity and pollution, whereas it is a matter of proscription for the Kiratas. For instance, the Angbhangs cannot kill or eat the pig; Khajums, the frog; Tumbapo, Tumbangphe and Labungma, the buffalo; *papona* (a particular type of fish), the Angdembe, Yekten and Lawati; *maksipa* (a black bird found in the streams), the Thamsuhang or Maksingbung; and goat, a number of clans like Lowa, Manglak, Nembeku, Younghang, Hangsurumba, Suhang, Jabegou, Kerung, Nembhang, Thegim and Yangsoma.

One of the stories explaining such restrictions is on why the Jabegous do not eat goat's meat: a Thegim ancestor (from whom the Jabegous have branched out) once married a dumb girl. While returning from her home, he received gifts of a broom, a goat and a cat. The couple had to cross the Koshi river and there were only a few strings of cane over it. The goat refused to cross; and his wife being dumb could not help to persuade it. He became very angry with the goat, and killed it, throwing its body into the river with this curse: "Let my descendants never eat your meat". The Jabegous thenceforth considered eating goat as a taboo.

In Chhinamakhu, the Rais worship a host of deities, three of which are most important. *Baktanchu* or the hearth god is worshipped after the harvest or in *Mangsir* (November–December) and is more popularly known as *Mangsire*. The new crop is offered to this god before it is eaten. *Homkumang* is considered the supreme god of energy and may be worshipped at any time of the year except June–July. *Satnanchinko* is the snake god and is considered to be an affinal deity but is propitiated inside the house by many. This indicates that the Rais do not maintain the distinction between consanguinal and affinal deities as strictly as the Limbus, at least in Yangnam, do (see note 1).

Satnanchinko is believed to cause paralysis, blindness and so on, if not propitiated properly, with the sacrifice of a hen (of any colour), ginger and liquor contained in a rice gourd laid on a make-shift altar and a *mangpa* or *nakchhong* to conduct the worship. *Chawamang* is the river god, which is worshipped by most Rais. There are also *Helamang* or the monkey god, *Samkimang* or the dog god, and many such deities representing different animals and birds, capable of causing different kinds of diseases.

However, it is noticed that the Rais have hardly any concept of proscription or taboo except among the Kwoyus who are not supposed to kill or eat goat though in practice many do.

The non-Kiratas in the village also worship various deities. Among the Tagadharis, for instance, the Chhetris worship *Bhimsen* or the ancestor god and *Kalanki* or the wind god with the sacrifice of male goats. Similarly, the Tamangs worship the wind god, which is believed to be borrowed originally from the Chhetris. Even the Untouchables worship their ancestor-god and *Bhimsen*, to which they sacrifice a cock (of any colour). Its blood is smeared on the stones erected as an altar inside the house. This takes place on the night of *Baisakh Purnima* or the full moon night of April–May.

The main deities among the Yakkhas in Madi Mulkharka are *Pangchyang* or the household god, *Yasokeni Boju* or the goddess of Yasok (a place near Fidim), and *Dhankute Devta*, which is called *Thungdangba* by the Limbus. Besides they have a host of affinal deities called *Minumachyang* or cat god, *Puchakchyang* or snake god, *Pubangchyang* or monkey god, *Kemma Samang* or ancestor god, *Maumachyang* or forest god, *Mangmechyang* or eagle god and so on.

For *Pangchyang*, a temporary altar is erected and decorated with a cock of any colour but certainly with porcupine-like feathers, flowers, fruits, one egg and tubers. It can be propitiated at any time of the year except on Sundays. The *Dhankute Devta* is considered to be the god of energy. To worship this deity, four or eight chickens and a goat, some *cireta* (the bitter herb), an egg and eight bamboo containers are used. This worship can take place at any time except on Sundays, during periods of mourning, and when a woman has just delivered a child at home.

The restriction on Sundays is understandable in view of their belief in another important god called *Aitabare* or the god who reigns on Sundays. Worshipping *Dhankute Devta* on Sundays may offend this deity. But restriction during mourning or childbirth can perhaps be attributed to the influence of the Tagadhari concept of purity and pollution. A female piglet is reared in the name of the goddess of Yasok and sacrificed when it grows big enough. At this deity's altar is kept about half a kilogram of rice, a *diyo* or small earthen lamp, and a *kalash* or a small copper pitcher. Riches may also be displayed at the altar. This deity too is not propitiated on Sundays. If angry, the deity is believed to be capable of causing the birth of physically and/or mentally handicapped babies.

To worship the cat god, the *phedangma* draws the picture of a human face on a piece of paper with charcoal and keeps these articles near it: a couple of coins, milk, rice, *ghee* and *achheta* or rice grains. All these are later collected and left at the crossroads. Failure to please it is believed to cause heartache or heartburn. In the case of the snake god, a snake-like figure is made with the help of flour and placed on a banana leaf with liquor and bread. If angry, this deity is believed to cause polio-like symptoms among children. Similarly, other deities are worshipped either to avoid various diseases or to propitiate them when the *phedangma* prophesises that someone is ill due to the ire of a particular deity.

As in the case of the Rais, the Yakkhas do not have taboos except among the Pinuhang and Morahang clans which cannot kill or eat buffalo. Other clans have no such proscriptions, but the Nechali, Amchoke and Mang-pang Rais do not eat goat.

Other categories in the village worship a host of deities like the *kul devta* or ancestor god, the gods of the river, the household, the wind, and the cowshed besides those worshipped by the Yakkhas like *Yasokeni Boje* and *Dhankute*. Except by the Bahuns, all other castes and communities sometimes undertake blood sacrifices of chickens, goats or pigs. Further, such worship occurs mainly twice a year, during *udhauli* and *ubhauli*. Other auspicious occasions are full-moon days and *Vijayadashami*.

Every caste or clan has some deities which have come from other clans or communities and other deities that are considered to be their own. The important deities require to be worshipped with the help of a formal priest but most deities are believed to be happy with the offerings or sacrifices made by the head of the household. In all such offerings, the leaves of banana, *Cynadon dactylon*, *Thysanolemma maxima*, *Castonopsis* and *Machilus* are considered sacred. Other sacred articles are the *achheta* rice grains, fire, incense of dry pine leaves, fruits and flowers. In certain cases, where the gender of the deity is well defined, offerings of birds and animals of the same gender are adhered to strictly. For instance, the *Theba Samang* is never offered a female pig, goat or chicken and the *Yuma Samang* a male animal or bird.

There are certain social implications attached to the association with such deities. Families with certain deities like the wind god, snake god, or monkey god are feared and matrimonial alliances with them are avoided. Such families avoid mentioning their deities but people in the village are aware of their association. Those harbouring such deities have problems, particularly in getting their daughters married and this compels them to look for spouses in distant villages.

In the villages of east Nepal, even the Bahuns had the practice of blood sacrifice in earlier times but it was later abandoned. For instance, the *kul devta* or ancestor god and *goth puja* or worshipping of the cowshed deity involved blood sacrifice earlier but today, only flowers, fruit and a few other such articles are offered. The practice of erecting temporary altars of mud, stones and banana trunks was also not confined to the Kiratas but was found among the Tagadharis and Other Mongoloids.

These are a few instances of religious syncretism one notices in the villages of east Nepal as well as in Darjeeling and Sikkim. The next chapter shows how they were bound together by a number of major deities like Durga, Vishnu and Mahadev (Shiva) besides the common festivals like *Dashain*, *Tihar*, and *Maghe Sankranti*.

The religion of the Tagadharis was not confined to certain scriptures but also incorporated deities specific to their place of migration. The realm of the oral religion of the Tagadharis thus fuses with that of the Kiratas and Other Mongoloids and overlaps that of the Untouchables. It is often forgotten that the written Hindu texts appropriated today by the Tagadharis are not things that have emerged from the blue. They are simply textualisations of religious practices which existed in oral form for thousands of years and which were shared by a large number of people before they were put down in writing.

Similarly, to call the Kiratas 'animists' would amount to only a partial representation of their religious beliefs and practices as much as representing the Tagadharis as Hindus. Such an effort would, at another plane, mean the imposition of inadequate, ill-defined concepts of realities which are far more diverse than the concepts representing them would have us believe. In post-modernist parlance, such efforts are meta-narrative efforts which ignore the minor, local, native contours of a culture. Such practices involve totalising the categories of culture and ignore the sublimated, the subjugated, the divergent and the local voices even within the dominant category.

The present discussion on culture, language and religion of the Kiratas vis-à-vis the Tagadharis in particular and other categories in general does not provide a very optimistic picture of these emerging as powerful symbols of Kirata nationalism. There are only a few isolated elements of the Kirata culture, language and religion which can be considered absent among the Tagadharis and even fewer among other categories. But the Kiratas cannot afford to ignore those elements which have, for various historical and other reasons, already fused with those found among other categories. If they do so, they carry with them only a part of what actually belongs to them. Abandoning some features just because they are shared by the Tagadharis would, in short, amount to lopping off its branches and threatening the very survival of the tree. But this perhaps cannot be helped in a nation-building operation which involves a process of internal homogenisation and external differentiation at national as well as nation-state levels.

The Kirata efforts at imagining their nationalism should perhaps concentrate more on emotional, attitudinal, or psychological unity rather than on rebuilding their culture, language and religion. For such a unity, they need not abandon the Nepali language to whose growth they have contributed so much in the past and are still contributing. Nor is it correct to brand the Nepali language as the language of the Tagadharis only. It is not really practical, after so much of nourishing by the Kiratas to abandon it on the plea that they were nurturing someone else's baby! It is, as a matter of fact, a common baby of the Kiratas, Other Mongoloids, Tagadharis and the Untouchables. Rather, they should try and take the help of this baby to achieve what they want. Similarly, abandoning Hinduism, no matter what this concept actually stands for, is perhaps fruitful only if it serves their all-round purpose—not merely the political.

NOTES

1. It should be clarified that this division exists only at the family and clan levels. It is not possible at the level of community because what is consanguinal to one clan can be affinal to another. From this it can be concluded that these deities can little hope to emerge as symbols at the national or even community level.

2. Some of these deities are:
   Asek Samang = snake god
   Saba Samang = monkey god
   Taksangba = hunter's god
   Pung Samang = hunter's god
   Chokhoba = sun god
   Tutulima = wind god
   Maya Samang = eagle god
   Kudhap Samang = forest god
   Mudenba Samang = Bhutia god

Politics of Kirata Culture

The destabilisation of the Kiratas began in 1641 in Sikkim with the establishment of the Namgyal dynasty, and in 1774 in Nepal after the subjugation of the Kirata kingdoms by Prithivinarayan Shah. Gradually, bit by bit, they lost their political autonomy, their *kipat*, their language, their religion and their culture. Those who migrated to Darjeeling and Sikkim even lost their traditional identity as they tried to adjust themselves to new environments.

Now, at the close of the twentieth century, they find they have moved too far away from their 'golden' past. It is only recently that a 'replay' of their past is becoming popular and even receiving mass approval. Though some of the players in this act may be nurturing some secret political ambitions, as most mainstream scholars would like to believe, their efforts towards this may also be read as a fight against the systems of domination as well as a positive direction towards state formation.

This fight is in many ways an unequal one. Though the people whom they are fighting are numerically small they have behind them a hegemonic state and a very strong "official discourse" by which Burton and Carlen mean "the systemization of modes of argument that proclaim the state's legal and administrative rationality" (1979:48). This discourse has been maintained by a section of the privileged class of Tagadharis because it is essential "not only to achieve the political incorporation of the dominated classes" but also to "sustain the confidence and knowledge of the hegemonic factions" (1979:48). The fight becomes more prohibitive for the subjugated communities when one considers the arguments that engulf them. In other words, they not only have to fight against the Tagadhari rulers at the state level but also against their own brethren who have so far remained part of the discourse created by the Tagadharis.

This discourse is not only hegemonic but also all-pervading. The marginalised nations like the Kiratas, for instance, question their own systems of belief and traditional practices. During fieldwork in Dungra village, Kalimpong, I encountered one scholarly Limbu who propounded a theory to explain their backwardness: "The Limbus are backward because they drink and eat the entrails of the pig much against the teachings of their *mundhum* but the words of which have been interpreted to suit their alcoholic and non-vegetarian tastes." That alcoholism is the main cause of their backwardness was also considered true by many elders in east Nepal. Citing Franz Fanon, Kuper remarks:

> ... the colonized were brought to admit that their misfortune resulted directly from their racial and cultural characteristics, and that they tried to escape the guilt and inferiority they experienced by proclaiming total and unconditional adoption of the new cultural models and irreversible condemnation of their own (1974:18).

It may be worthwhile here to refer to Dilli Ram Dahal to whom a doctorate was awarded by the University of Hawaii in 1983. His thesis is an example of how such a discourse is kept alive by Tagadhari academia. His view, based on the Athpahariya Rais of east Nepal, is that the Kiratas had plenty of land earlier and were rich but they did not bother to educate their children. Instead they indulged in alcoholism and lavish lifestyles. Eventually they lost their land and became poor—an explanation which not only pleases the hegemonic class but also seems to satisfy the subordinate categories.

A welcome exception to the studies perpetuating this theory is *Fatalism and Development* by Dor Bahadur Bista (1991). This work is compared by Alan Macfarlane (1993:93), though perhaps a little unjustifiably, with Tocqueville's *Ancient Regime*, Weber's *Protestant Ethic*, and Taine's *Notes Upon England*. The essential idea in Bista's book is as follows:

> The current nature of Nepali society is such that the groups with positive elements of value systems in their social and collective practices are increasingly excluded from the mainstream of society and their values are endangered as another, essentially alien, culture becomes more pervasive. This other culture, the culture of fatalism, includes values and institutions that are inherently in conflict with development (Bista 1991:2).

The contention in this passage may be more transparent if we understand what he means by 'culture of fatalism'. According to him, it refers to

'Bahunism', which is a concept used essentially to refer to the socio-political behaviour of the Brahmans of the middle hills. 'Brahmanism' would be too broad a concept and would include the terai Brahmans as well, which would distort the reality because the latter have little or no control over the state apparatus. One must admire his courage in saying so, given the socio-political and academic scenario of Nepal.

Symbols of Unity or Difference?

The Kiratas of the eastern Himalayas are today suffering from a lack of national symbols which would represent them and simultaneously differentiate them from the Tagadharis and also the Untouchables whose culture is so similar to that of the Tagadharis. The question of difference with Other Mongoloids is perhaps the most vexing one for various reasons. Many Kirata leaders are aware of the fact that their fight against the Tagadhari hegemony in Nepal is bound to be unsuccessful without the support of the Other Mongoloids. They are aware of some cultural and linguistic differences between them but they also know that the similarities are more. Hence they are in a difficult situation, unable to clearly decide whether to give primacy to similarities or differences with other categories. This ambivalence is clearly noticeable in their politics.

It is important for the Kiratas to construct powerful symbols of difference with the Tagadharis for it is mainly the latter whom they hold responsible for their present state of affairs. It is again the latter against whom they occur to be fighting. But this fight is rather uneasy: the symbols of difference between them are not as powerful as the Kirata leaders would like them to be. Interaction between these two categories for over two hundred years now has made the symbols of difference less powerful than either category would perhaps like. Though they are socially quite different and psychologically perhaps a little more so, other facts of their lives and living such as economic interdependence, language, dress, ecology and destiny bind them together rather than separate them. Retreating to an ideal and convenient past to construct the symbols of difference is common but in no way easy for the Kiratas.

The search for such a 'past' is a tedious task for nations trying to build themselves anew. The process of nation-building requires cultural and ideological homogenisation of the people belonging or claiming to belong to a nation, as it is so in the case of nation-building at the level of the nation-state. But the condition of Kirata affairs at present is such that they are not sure what the premises on which to base such cultural and ideological homogenisation should be. The efforts have just begun but consensus may evade them for a while yet.

To begin with, the *kipat* system and the *mundhum* are traditionally uncontested metaphors of Kirata culture. Similarly, the worshipping of *Tagera Nyingmaphuma* or the supreme deity was a pan-Kirata symbol. But with the abolition of the *kipat* system and the simultaneous influence of Hinduism, these symbols have lost their strength considerably. Since *Tagera Nyingmaphuma* is often personified as *Shiva*, who is not only considered a tribal god but also one of the Hindu pantheon, he cannot be claimed by the Kiratas as their exclusive god.

The Sirijanga script has been referred to as the Kirata script and promoted as a Kirata symbol for quite some time now. With regard to its linguistic status, Keith Sprigg, an authority on Tibeto-Burman languages, writes that this script has some resemblance to the Devanagari "but in general the resemblance seems closest to a Tibetan cursive (*'khyug-yig*) and Lepcha. In particular, the Kiranti script shares with these two the feature of having a special series of letters for syllable-final consonants" (IOL MSS Eur D 537). However, most Rais of Sikkim as well as Nepal tend to consider this script a 'Limbu' and not a 'Kiranti script'.

The Rais have a real problem of linguistic homogenisation as the dialectical diversity is colossal (see Hanpon 1991). The Limbus too have some dialectical variations (see Driem 1987:xvii–xix, Weidert and Subba 1985:4–7) but these are not as great as in the case of the Rais. The problems of their linguistic diversity were discussed in the international Rai convention held in March 1992 at Jhapa, Nepal. It was finally decided not to pursue linguistic homogenisation. It is quite understandable at this stage of nation-building among the Rais because the emotional attachment to their respective dialects and localities is still strong and a standardisation programme now might divide them ideologically. But at a later stage, the Bantawa dialect has great potential to emerge as a link language for the Rais. This dialect is not only believed to be easy to speak and understand, but it is already used by a large majority of them.

Many Kiratas have now begun to name their children in their own languages rather than in Nepali. Some of them have stopped inviting Brahman priests to officiate at the naming ceremony. Similarly, many who gave alms in the form of rice, lentils, money, and so on to the Jogis who visited every house at night chanting *mantras* and blowing conch shells have stopped entertaining them. Though it is doubtful if this enthusiasm will be sustained, such efforts have the potential to become strong symbols of their difference. But they may also contribute to the furtherance of cultural differences among the Kiratas themselves.

Some Kiratas have more or less resolved that the *Dashain*, which they celebrated with all enthusiasm till a couple of years ago, is not a Kirata festival. This festival, known elsewhere as *Durga Puja* is one in which Durga, the goddess of strength, is worshipped. But one must note the differences between the ways in which the Kiratas (and some Other Mongoloid communities) and Tagadharis (and Untouchables) celebrate it. For the latter categories, it continues for a fortnight in October but for the former categories the important day is only the tenth or *Vijayadashami* On this day they receive blessings from their parents, grandparents and senior relatives in the form of *tika*, some coins and flowers. In turn, the younger or junior kins touch the feet of the elders in obeisance. This is followed by feasting till late in the evening.

Further, the Tagadharis pronounce a definite *mantra* (Vedic verse) at the time of blessing the junior kins but such a *mantra* is rarely uttered by the Kiratas. The latter never use the name of any Hindu deity in the blessing but usually use these words: "May your descendants swarm the hills and gorges; may the enemies feel scared of you; may you be able to help your parents, relatives and friends..."

Thus, the *Dashain* of the Kiratas may be considered to be functionally and symbolically different from the *Dashain* of the Tagadharis for whom it is more a religious occasion whereas for the former it is primarily a get-together of relatives, or a social occasion. In other words, there is, perhaps, no reason why the Kiratas should abandon this festival as has been done in many places in Darjeeling, Sikkim and east Nepal since 1991.

Tihar is another important festival which has been 'invented' on the authority of their *mundhum* to be of Kirata content. This festival is also known as *Dipawali* or 'festival of lights' and Lakshmi Puja or worship of Lakshmi, the goddess of wealth. This occurs about a fortnight after *Dashain*.

During this festival, the Kiratas and others alike clean and white-wash or daub/paint their houses. They also decorate their houses with flowers and plantain trees. Then young men and women go from house to house singing eulogies of the legendary king, Bali Raja, who is believed to have been a Kirata. Legend has it that this king was so generous that he gave away everything, including the piece of land on which he was standing, to a *rishi* or saint who first asked for land just enough for three paces. But his stride turned out to be so great that his three paces covered not only the sky and *patal* or land below the earth, but also this earth. Since the king had already given his word to the *rishi*, he had no option but to disappear into *patal* and fulfil his promise. (This story has resemblances to that of the Onam festival in Kerala in south India and is symbolic of the Aryan usurpation of indigenous resources after they migrated to India.) The festival called *Gai Tihar* or the festival of the cow begins two days before the *Dipawali* or new moon night. Prior to that they have *Kag Tihar* and *Kukur Tihar* or the festivals of the crow and the dog respectively. The day after *Gai Tihar* is called *Goru Tihar* or the festival of the ox. On the fifth day is *Bhaitika* when sisters, consanguineous or fictitious, wish their brothers, own or classificatory, long lives by putting *tika* on their foreheads and garlanding them. In return, the brothers touch the feet of their sisters and make gifts of money before they are offered food and drink by the sisters.

Thus, except for the singing of eulogies of Bali Hang or Bali Raja, there is nothing specific that can be described as being of Kirata content. The worship of domestic animals like the cow, ox, or dog was not only part of the Aryan tradition but even today there is a close cultural association with these animals. The cow, in particular, assumes a sacred place as an object of worship for the Aryans if not for other categories as well.

The festival which may perhaps be more accurately called 'Kirata' is *Maghe Sankranti*, which falls in the middle of January every year. Though the name of this festival is of Indo-Aryan origin it is necessary to observe its details. On this day, the Kiratas make it a point to take a ceremonial bath before eating boiled roots and tubers collected from the forests and fields or purchased from the market. Then they go to the river banks or confluences to make blood sacrifices in fulfillment of the promises made to certain deities when someone in the family had taken ill. Even the Tagadharis participate in this festival but instead of making sacrifices they, as also some Rais, set a pair of pigeons free. All this shows that the festival is of tribal origin but as of now all Hindu Nepalis celebrate and participate enthusiastically in it.

Coming to dance forms, the *Sakkewa* or *Chandi Nach* of the Rais, and *Yalang* or *Dhan Nach* and *Kelang* or *Chyabhrung Nach* of the Limbus and Yakkhas are important and are being promoted as their cultural symbols. The *Sakkewa* dance, which is also a festival, is performed at the time of the full moon of *Baisakh* (April–May) and is understandably devoted to the rain deity. Water from all directions is collected in a rice gourd and the villagers assemble at the main source of water before the dance dedicated to this deity begins. Only drums and cymbals are used. According to Tirtha Raj Rai, President of Bhojpur district Kirant Rai Yayokkha, there are mainly three *silees* or patterns of the *Sakkewa* dance. They are *(1)* agricultural operations like sowing seeds, transplanting the seedlings, harvesting and threshing; *(2)* craft-related work (basket making for males and sowing of cotton seeds or weaving for females), and *(3)* mimicry of the birds flying in the sky. However, he regrets that nowadays *Sakkewa* dancers also mimic the rubbing of tobacco and lime on their palms, which indicates a degeneration in its sacred content. Normally, each performance continues for about three hours and is concluded with a devotion to their supreme deities called Sumnima (or Parvati) and Paruhang (or Shiva). (For details, see Koyu 1992 and Walakhamcha 1992.)

The *Yalang* begins in December after the crops are harvested and continues till February or so. However, in Yangnam such dance could be seen being performed even in May. This, according to some villagers, is something new and disturbing to them. It is probably due to the lack of sacred content in this dance and also because it provides opportunities for courtship and entertainment.

In the *Sakkewa* festival, a *mangpa* or priest must guide the dance group and make a sacrifice of goats to the rain deity at the *Sakkewa Than* or altar. As a matter of fact, there is no altar in the true sense of the word: what one sees are a couple of iron tridents and stones erected vertically in the corner of a ground which becomes a sacred area during this dance. But neither a priest nor any such sacrifice is necessary for *Yalang* or the *Kelang*. Further, unlike in the *Kelang*, which is performed only by men, *Yalang* and *Sakkewa* are essentially meant for both men and women. But there is a culturally significant difference between the last two: while men and women lock their elbows and dance with a vigorous swing in the former, they are not supposed to touch each other in the latter. Finally, the former involves no hand gestures whereas in the latter, this is the most important aspect of the entire show.

On closer scrutiny, these dance forms show that the Khambus were dependent on agriculture from much earlier times than the other two Kirata communities. That the Limbus and Yakkhas were more dependent on pastoralism and hunting than agriculture is indicated by the complete absence of the rain deity or any other cultural expression of such like among them. But, according to James Clifford, traditions "need not take root in ancestral plots; they live by pollination, by (historical) transplanting" (1988:15). The Kiratas have perhaps not yet indulged in such transplantation but they may need to do so if the original roots fail to take them where they want to go.

Such efforts at 'inventing' the symbols of unity/difference are seldom smooth and they are bound to alienate some members of the community. If Tagadhari efforts at cultural homogenisation have alienated a large number of non-Tagadhari communities in Nepal, such efforts of the Kiratas are also alienating certain sections of their own people. This is perhaps inevitable, because any 'invention of tradition' involves the imposition of the values and ideologies of a section of people over others. Such values and ideologies are not new but already existing in a culture, nor is the forcing of these upon the masses something new. It has always happened in history, and repeatedly so. Hobsbawm rightly points out that 'invented tradition' is after all "a set of practices, normally governed by overtly or tacitly accepted rules and of a ritual or symbolic nature, which seek to inculcate certain values and norms of behaviour by repetition, which automatically implies continuity with the past" (1984:1).

Kirata culture and identity are in fact suffering from the pangs of being (re)born as a historical necessity which has arisen out of a situation dominated heavily by a culture which they now find difficult to dissociate from. Whether these are signs of nation-building or nation-breaking remains for posterity to tell.

Kirata Politics

Though Caplan (1970) has documented Kirata politics in east Nepal from the late eighteenth century till the late 1960s, his data do not relate to the Khambus and Yakkhas nor has anyone else written about their post-Gorkha politics. But it is difficult to assume that they did not protest at the Gorkha exploitation and subordination. However, this is a historical gap which remains to be filled.

It appears from Caplan's study that the politics of the Limbus of east Nepal was mainly centred around the interests of the *kipat* holders. There was no permanent political association nor any leader to give a clear direction. It was mainly based on ad hoc committees of Subbas and apparently directed against certain legislations of the country which threatened their interests. A close reading of their movement, however, reveals that they were not only trying to protect their *kipat* holdings but the very symbol of their culture and identity. But being "uncoordinated and ill-organised", they could do very little. The only achievement, according to Caplan, was to build up "internal solidarity and differentiation from other groups" (1970:188). This is, however, no small matter in its own merit and particularly in view of the prevailing socio-political situation then. The revolution of 1950 in which the Kiratas made an effort to physically drive away the Tagadharis from east Nepal, leading to the destruction of their life and property in many villages, may be taken as ventilation of Kirata anger against the Tagadharis. But this would not have been possible had not the cleavage between them developed from the late eighteenth century itself.

The present trend of their politics is rather complex and ambivalent. They are not only forming and actively supporting organisations which may be called 'tribal' but also, though without any sense of contradiction, participating in such organisations which are pan-Kirata, pan-Nepali and even transnational. As of now, there is only one clear idea, that is, that their common enemy is the Bahuns in particular and Tagadharis in general. But they are not yet clear about how they will overcome their enemy and what *ashtras* or weapons to use for this. Hence, they are experimenting with various kinds such as 'Kirata', 'Mongoloid', 'Janajati'. Whether they will ultimately choose one or a combination of these remains to be seen. However, until now, the concept 'Kirata' does not seem to be accepted as an effective weapon by all Kiratas and it is difficult to say if this will evolve as a powerful symbol or rallying point in the future.

In this context, it is perhaps worthwhile to give a profile of various organisations in Darjeeling, Sikkim and Nepal in which the Kiratas are participating fully or partly. Not all are Kirata organisations but their participation in all of them is significant and therefore justifies their being discussed here within the purview of Kirata politics.

1. Lhomentsongsum: A 'treaty' in the mid-seventeenth century among the Lhopas (Bhutias), Monpas (Lepchas) and Tsongs (Limbus) of Sikkim, Lhomentsongsum stands for the trio of Lhopas, Monpas and Tsongs. It was an enactment of a blood relationship among these three indigenous communities of Sikkim, with the first as father, the second as mother, and the last as son. The historical testimony to this ritual consanguinity can still be found at a place called Kabi Lungchok in north Sikkim.

This treaty was understandably to ensure the stability of the Namgyal dynasty in the first few decades after 1641 when it faced a threat from both the Lepchas and the Limbus. But it did not lose significance even after this dynasty was fully established. A new need to keep it alive was felt due to the migration of people from Nepal during the late nineteenth century, threatening the demographic balance of Sikkim. Thus, it became the symbol of identity for the indigenous Sikkimese.

Over the years, the community which seems most disillusioned with this treaty is the Limbu. Due to their identification with the Nepalis, the other two communities did not extend support when the reserved seat for the Limbus in the State Assembly was withdrawn in 1974 and they failed to muster support for the scheduled tribe status in 1978. They have ventilated their grievances to the appropriate authorities from time to time though without success so far. For instance, a lengthy memorandum dated 5 November 1981 was submitted to the Prime Minister of India through the then Chief Minister of Sikkim, Nar Bahadur Bhandari, by sixty prominent Limbu leaders and three members of the Sikkim Legislative Assembly. In this memorandum, reference has been made to Lhomentsongsum, the cultural distinctiveness of the Limbus, and their overall backwardness in the fields of education and development, and their political voicelessness. It concludes with an appeal to recognise them as a scheduled tribe (*Sikkim Observer*, hereafter SO 7/1987).

An appeal for the revision of the list of scheduled tribes in Sikkim and inclusion of the Limbu community in it was once again made on 14 June 1990 in a memorandum submitted to the President of India by a delegation of Limbus and other tribal groups under the banner of Akhil Sikkim Kirat Limboo Chumlung. Reference to Lhomentsongsum is also made in this memorandum along with other historical references establishing their antiquity in Sikkim (SO 7/1990).

Under the prime ministership of V P Singh, a list of Other Backward Classes (OBCs) of Sikkim was prepared, which included the Limbus, Rais, Mangars, Gurungs, Tamangs and Bhujels (C'wang 1990). By then, the Limbus had resolved to accept the OBC status but the State Government headed by Nar Bahadur Bhandari refused to implement the Mandal Commission recommendations (SO 8/1990).

2. *Sarva Kiranti Chumlung*: The All Kirata Council was established on 26 July 1925 initially as Hang Chumlung or a 'council of kings' at Dungra village, Kalimpong, in order to propagate 'knowledge' among the Limbus and to develop their language. Laliswor Sendang, an 84-year-old Limbu had been living since 1911 at Kolbung Alainchibari cave to escape arrest and persecution by the Rana rulers in Nepal. He moved to Dungra for four years between 1926 and 1930 to teach and propagate the Limbu language and culture.

It was only at the fifty-first Annual General Conference of this Council held on 25 December 1976 that it was renamed Sarva Kiranti Chumlung and the rules and regulations framed in 1925 were amended so that other

Kirata communities could also join and strengthen it. The minutes of the meetings held after that were recorded in the Devanagari script instead of the earlier Sirijanga script.

But the effort to accommodate members of other Kirata communities have not met with any success. It has still remained largely a Limbu council as only a couple of members from the Rai and Gurung communities have joined it. Difficulties have also arisen due to the geographical distribution of its members over Darjeeling, Sikkim, Assam and Nepal. The contents of the files in its office further show that the working of this Council was obstructed by the police both in Sikkim and Nepal.

3. All India Kirat Chumlung Association Sabha: Initially a branch of the Hang Chumlung established in Kalimpong in July 1925, it was only after the All India Kirat Chumlung Association Sabha's reorganisation under this new name on 26 September 1971 that it began to function actively.

This Association was fortunate to have received the guidance and patronage of Iman Singh Chemjong from 1931 to 1976. But due to his long absences from Darjeeling at the School of Oriental and African Studies in London and Tribhuwan University in Kathmandu, his services were not always available. It actually got a new lease of life only after Surya Kumari Chemjong, a teacher at Turnbull High School, Darjeeling, agreed to be its general secretary in 1980.

Now there are problems due to differences between the Rai and Limbu members. The Rai members are not happy with the word 'Chumlung' attached to the name of this Association as they consider it to be a Limbu word whereas the Limbus, who are the main office-bearers, seem adamant about retaining it. Nor are the Rais particularly pleased with the *Kelang* and *Yalang* dance programmes organised by the Association. The attitude of the Rais is important because numerically they constitute the majority of members. Thus, unless the Limbu office-bearers become a little more accommodative of the ethos and aspirations of their Rai compatriots, the future of this Association seems gloomy.

4. Akhil Sikkim Kirat Limbu Chumlung: The Akhil Sikkim Kirat Limbu Chumlung was established on 23 May 1973 at a place called Tharpu in West Sikkim. The first general meeting of this Council was held at Soreng Bazaar in West Sikkim on 19 July 1973 under the chairmanship of H. D. Chong. One of the important resolutions passed at this meeting (Resolution No 8) was that the 'Chongs' were not 'Nepalis' but one of the indigenous tribes of Sikkim (see Chemjong 1973:34–40 for details).

The first major activity of this Council seems to be its submission of a memorandum dated 14 June 1990 to the President of India demanding the "[i]nclusion of the Limboo community in Sikkim in the schedule[d] tribe list of the state". This memorandum was signed by, among others, Sanchaman Limboo, then a member of the Assembly and ruling Sikkim Sangram Parishad (and later Chief Minister for a brief period), and Birbal Subba, then a minister in Bhandari's cabinet. For this 'audacity' of theirs, they had to face a 'show cause' notice served by Bhandari asking why they had signed it without his consent.

K. B. Subba, the general secretary of this Council, issued a press release demanding the resignation of Bhandari for having retracted from his earlier commitment to help the Limbus obtain scheduled tribe status (SO 11/1990). In another press release issued by him in February 1991 he reiterated the Council's demand for restoration of the Limbu seat in the Assembly as prior to 1974 and recognition of the Limbus as a scheduled tribe (SO 2/1991).

Apart from such demands made from time to time, this Council has also addressed itself to the question of Limbu culture and identity. For instance, the memorandum of 14 June 1990 says:

> At this juncture, the community [Limbu] is facing a threat of losing the purity of its language and culture. The various factors and forces through which they have traversed so far have already diluted their life patterns pushing them to utter submission and dependence. Now they are threatened of their very identity (SO 7/1990).

5. *Sirijanga Yakthung Sakthim Phochumpo* (Sirijanga Limbu Cultural Organisation): Established in 1976–77 and registered in August 1980, the Sirijanga Yakthung Sakthim Phochumpo was founded by a Mohan Ijam of Lingchong, West Sikkim. Its founding office-bearers and executive members were all farmers (except one who was a contractor) from Tharpu, West Sikkim. Incidentally, all the office-bearers belonged to the Khewa clan while the executive members belonged to the Nembhang clan.

Such a mono or dual clan or occupational composition was slightly diversified in the committees constituted subsequently in 1987 and 1990. These committees then had members from Tharpu, Hee Bermiok, Lingchong and the Uttare areas of West Sikkim as well.

It is too early to assess its achievements but its objectives are clear—to restore and develop the Limbu culture through research and propagation of its cultural heritage like *Yalang* and *Kelang*.

6. Kirant Dharma Tatha Sahitya Utthan Sangh (Kirata Religion and Literature Development Association): This Kirata Association was established in 1979 at Fidim, the district headquarters of Panchthar. The objectives of this Association not only include the development of their religion and literature but also their language, script and culture. Though it is supposed to be a pan-Kirata association, the Limbus dominate its central committee as well as its branch committees at Jhapa and Lalitpur.

One of its greatest achievements is perhaps the establishment of a Kirat Press at Damak in the terai of Nepal. This is a feat which the Kirata associations of Darjeeling and Kalimpong have not been able to manage in the last seven decades or so. This has made it possible for leaflets, pamphlets and books on Kirata religion and culture to be published.

The Association seeks to propagate a religion called 'Kirant Dharma' but what it is propagating is better described as Satyehangma Dharma, a *bhakti* (devotional) cult founded by Mahaguru Swami Phalgunanda, a Limbu ascetic born of a poor farmer in 1885 at a village called Chukchinamba in the Ilam district of east Nepal. Besides preaching *bhakti* as the only way to reach God, this Dharma preaches other things which are of great importance to Kirata culture and religion. Among them are:

a. to avoid unnecessary expenses at the time of birth, marriage and death;
b. not to take bride-price;
c. not to quarrel or tell lies;
d. to give up alcoholism and non-vegetarianism;
e. not to indulge in theft and *jari* (marrying another's wife);
f. to provide equal educational opportunities to sons and daughters.

(For details, see Kainla 1990:xvii–xxi)

Of all these teachings, the most objectionable to many Limbus not belonging to this sect is the fourth. Those who do not subscribe to this Dharma argue strongly that if they follow all these teachings they will in no way be different from the Chhetri-Bahuns. But such a difference of opinion has not as yet mattered much because even the followers of this Dharma do not practise these teachings seriously nor do they insist on non-alcoholism or vegetarianism. This Dharma has certain other positive aspects. For instance, all the hymns of this Dharma are sung in the Limbu language and they are dedicated to Tagera Nyingmaphuma, the supreme deity of all Kiratas. This makes it different from other *bhakti* cults prevalent in Nepal and India like the Kabir Panthi, Pranami Dharma, Josmani Sant Dharma and so on.

7. *Limbuan Mukti Morcha* (Limbuan Liberation Front): Though this Limbuan Mukti Morcha was established by Bir Nembhang on 20 December 1986, it was not known beyond the region until he circulated its manifesto published on 18 January 1989 (Nembhang 1991:8). Still it is not known exactly where it is located or who its members are. Sometimes alleged to be a creation of Indians (see *Aaloke* 1988) and sometimes to be an associate organisation of the United Marxist–Leninist Party (see *Naba Pravah* 1991), its credentials are questioned by many. It was perhaps for this reason that its president, Bir Nembhang, was imprisoned soon after the publication of its manifesto and released in 1990.

It may be recalled here that a similar organisation called *Prachanda Gorkha* was formed in 1931 in Kathmandu, allegedly with the aid of "Indian terrorists" (Rose and Fisher 1970:94). The role of external powers in autonomy movements such as *Prachanda Gorkha* has also been pointed out by Howard Erdman (1979:405–06).

Several allegations have been made against this Limbuan Liberation Front by the Nepalese media which is absolutely controlled by the Tagadharis. It is branded as 'extremist' and 'anti-national'. But if the manifesto of this Front is to be taken into consideration, most such allegations, raised invariably by Tagadhari editors and reporters, are exaggerated, even concocted. Its demand, simply put, is "autonomy" and within the framework of the nation-state of Nepal, which this Front considers as an a priori condition for the development of the Limbu "script, language, religion, culture, art and civilisation" (SO 5/1989). There seems nothing wrong about it.

A lengthy letter dated 20 June 1990 written by Bir Nembhang and published in *Mechi Pravah* (1990) indicates that it has slightly modified its main claim, which it now calls a 'protectorate' state, though within the nation-state of Nepal. In a leaflet dated 1 June 1992, its president further revised the Front's demand to include the areas west of the Teesta within the territory of Limbuan.

8. *Mongol National Organisation*: The Mongol National Organisation was founded on 1 January 1989 by Gopal Gurung during his imprisonment at Bhadragol Jail, Kathmandu, reportedly for having published the now banned book titled *Nepali Rajnitima Adekha Sachai* (*Hidden Facts of Nepalese Politics*, 1985/1988). This book makes a powerful case for the Organisation and its demands and was widely read by most non-Tagadhari literate people of Darjeeling, Sikkim and Nepal.

The Organisation has a charter of 22 demands. The most important among them are: establishment of the multi-party system (which has already been effected); secularism; provision for provincial governments; teaching of all languages and scripts from Class I; replacement of Bikram Sambad with the Gregorian, Buddhist or Newari calendar reservation of 75% of seats in the Public Service Commission and other government establishments for the people of Mongol origin; no national dress; separate departments for untouchables and minorities; no change of village names without the concurrence of the majority in the village: legalising the eating of beef; and freedom of religion.

These are, in fact, not merely a charter of demands but actually old grievances. They also tell us the kind of subordination that existed and continues to exist in Nepal. It may not be possible for a country which is just groping towards democracy to accommodate all this, but the sooner the Nepalese Government realises their importance the better. Ignoring them persistently on various pleas or subverting the voices of those who raise such issues may only provide a temporary solution.

9. Kirant Yakthung Chumlung (Kirata Limbu Council): A meeting of about 150 Limbus living in various parts of Kathmandu decided in September 1989 that an organisation for the "promotion of Yakthung [Limbu] language, literature, and all-round development of the community" was needed. After three months, the constitution of the Kirant Yakthung Chumlung was ready and it was approved in its first conference held in Kathmandu on 6 January 1990.

From its *Chumlung Bulletin* published in Nepali as well as English, it appears that the council is functioning actively in holding seminars, talks and symposiums on various aspects of Limbu culture and tradition. It is in close association with various other organisations like the Mongol National Organisation, the Nepal Rastriya Janajati Morcha and the Mongol Kirant Janajati Utthan Manch.

Its location in Kathmandu has been advantageous for this Council especially with regard to propaganda. And in modern politics, as in business, a good campaign is half the battle won. But being located there has its disadvantages too: the usual danger of being close to the centre of power, the danger of being sabotaged, and the danger of being 'sold out'. Few can ignore power, career, job, promotion, privileges, foreign trips, and the Kiratas are, perhaps, no exceptions.

10. Kirat Rai Yayokkha (Kirat Rai Organisation): The outcome of a two-day conference of the Rais held in Kathmandu in 1990, the Kirat Rai

Organisation was finally established in 1991 with its headquarters in Kathmandu. It has a number of objectives, the most important of them being: unity among the Rais; preservation and development of their language, script, religion, art, culture; and cooperation with national and international organisations engaged in such activities (N. K. Rai 1992:1). But according to Tirtha Raj Rai, an important Rai leader and scholar, the main objectives as far as his district committee is concerned are: *(1)* promotion of *Chandi Nach*, *(2)* boycott of *Dashain*, *(3)* abstinence from smoking and drinking, and *(4)* gradual homogenisation [*ekrupta*] of the Rai cultures and languages.

Within a short period of two years, this Organisation has established branches in various districts of east Nepal and even village-level committees have been formed in some districts of Khambuan (N. K. Rai 1992:2). It has initiated the preparation of a comprehensive dictionary of the Rai languages. Efforts are also being made to get the *Sakkewa* festival recognised as a national festival in Nepal.

One of its most important achievements so far has been the organising of an international conference at Jhapa in March 1992. It was attended not only by prominent Rai and Limbu intellectuals and leaders from Nepal but also from Darjeeling, Sikkim, Assam and Meghalaya, besides some European scholars. At this conference, the consensus was not to homogenise their languages at this stage but to use the Devanagari script till a script of their own is developed to suit the phonetic peculiarities of their languages (N. K. Rai 1992).

Despite considerable linguistic and cultural variations across clans and regions, this Organisation has been able to make commendable progress. Given the educational and professional background of its patrons and leaders, it is likely to emerge as a major organisation of the Rais in the near future.

11. Akhil Kirant Rai Sangh of Sikkim: Established on 12 June 1990, the Akhil Kirant Rai Sangh has formed district and block level committees in Sikkim. The emergence of this Association is alleged to be due to certain misunderstandings between the Limbus and Rais of Sikkim. The Limbus have often enjoyed a special status in Sikkim as one of the three indigenous communities, a position which the Rais have not been able to enjoy despite being the single largest community there.

The Association was formed in order to develop the Rai language, promote their cultural traditions, bring about reforms in their lifestyles and strive for over-all socio-economic development. It is interesting to note here that they have taken *Dhan Nach*, which is simply a Nepali word for the Limbu *Yalang* as a part of their cultural tradition. As regards a script, the leaders are absolutely certain that they will not accept what is often described as the 'Kiranti' script.

The Rais of Sikkim have more challenges to meet towards the homogenisation of their language and culture than their brethren in Nepal. Most of them in Sikkim admit their total ignorance about their language and culture. They hope to revive their lost heritage with the help of a few surviving leaders who themselves differ on many issues of their language and culture. The invention of a script is not impossible when whole traditions are sometimes invented, but it is difficult to predict if that will serve their purpose functionally as well as symbolically.

12. Nepal Janajati Mahasangh (Nepal Federation of Nationalities): This Federation was established in July 1990 with the following associations as its constituent members:

1 Kirant Yakthung Chumlung
2 Kirant Rai Yayokkha
3 Chantyal Pariwar Sangh
4 Nepal Magar Sangh
5 Tamu Boudha Sewa Samiti
6 Nepal Bhasha Manka Khala
7 Tharu Kalyan Karini Sabha
8 Thakali Sewa Samiti
9 Sunuwar Sewa Samiti
10 Yahmbu Sherpa Chi-Chhog
11 Meche Samaj Sudhar Samiti
12 Nepal Hyolmo Samaj Sewa Sangh
13 Nepal Tamang Ghedung Sangh
14 Dhimal Jatiya Utthan Kendra
15 Rajbansi Bhasha Prachar Samiti
16 Danuwar (Jirel) Jagran Samiti
17 Niko Thami Sewa Samiti
18 Kirat Dharma Tatha Sahitya Utthan Sangh

(For details, see Fisher 1993:11–4)

The emergence of this Federation, an important landmark in the history of Nepal, has no parallels in Darjeeling and Sikkim. Without the ushering in of democracy there in 1990 this would have been unthinkable. But the fact that no such serious effort to bring solidarity among the politically and culturally suppressed groups has ever been witnessed in Darjeeling and Sikkim indicates that the situation in those regions is not as critical as the one in Nepal—despite a higher level of literacy, infrastructural development, and an older history of the emergence of such organisations. This could, however, be partly attributed to the composition of society in the latter regions, which is much more complex and heterogeneous than in Nepal. On the other hand, the situation in Nepal, at least organisationally, seems almost ripe for a consolidation of national priorities.

That the Tagadharis have not remained silent spectators to such development is evident from the scores of articles in newspapers and magazines published in Nepal as well as outside, and the formation of the Tagadhari Suraksha Samaj. Their anxiety and concern is also evident from a leaflet titled *Gayatri Mantra* published on behalf of the Tagadhari Suraksha Samaj, Rumtek Basti, East Sikkim in October 1992 by one Debnarayan Kharel (Bahun) and printed at Jai Jagadamba Offset, Varanasi. This leaflet calls upon the Tagadharis to rise up and demolish the ugly heads which the 'matwalis' are raising today. It says that 'others', meaning 'matwalis', are trying to wrest power and authority from the hands of the Tagadharis in Nepal and Sikkim. Quoting verses from the Gita, it says that they and they alone have the brain and the brawn to rule; others are meant to be at their feet, ruled for ever because they have emerged from the feet of Brahma. Finally, it calls upon Tagadharis to pull down any non-Tagadhari leader by hook or crook (*Sam*, *Dam*, *Danda*, *Vedh*).

This leaflet is meant for circulation strictly among the Tagadharis and it is marked "strictly confidential" but copies of it have spread among the Kiratas as well. The Kirata reaction, as also that of the Other Mongoloids, has, predictably, been furious, and many of them, who were non-committal before, have joined the politics of nationality after reading *Gayatri Mantra*.

Kirata politics, due to various social, political and historical reasons, seems to be evolving differently in Nepal and outside it. While, on the one hand, larger confederations based on 'Kirata', 'Mongol', or 'Janajati' identities are emerging in Nepal, even the Limbus and Rais have not been able to sort out their differences in Darjeeling and Sikkim. Community-level organisations are far more active and vigorous than the larger confederations even in Nepal. But there is also a tendency to go beyond the boundaries of communities in Nepal whereas in Darjeeling and Sikkim they appear to be retracting to their respective communal boundaries from the (earlier) national (Kirata) boundaries.

Apparently, all these organisations aim at a reshuffling of power at the level of the nation-state but, at a more abstract level, they want 'development' which is, of course, a concomitant of power under the nation-state framework. For development, most of the non-Tagadhari communities in Nepal seem to have the Indian system of constitutional protection of the rights of the scheduled castes, tribes and minorities at the back of their minds, though some organisations apparently would not settle for anything less than 'autonomous' statehood. There are some interstate organisations but their political agenda are set within the framework of existing nation-states. No organisation has as yet aired the demand for secession from the existing nation-state boundaries.

It is perhaps characteristic of an incipient nationalism that the various organisations are not able to clearly define and articulate their political goals. One often has to read between the lines in their leaflets, pamphlets and memoranda in order to discern what they want. And in doing so, one often tends to be obstructed by the garb of culture which sometimes appears to lack transparency.

The chapter on Kirata politics will perhaps be incomplete without a brief discussion on Kirata factionalism.

In Nepal, there is not only a lack of cooperation but also of communication among the leaders of the various Kirata organisations. Each claims to be the real messiah and alleges that the others are stooges of the government.

During the last parliamentary elections in Jhapa, there was stone-throwing between the supporters of the Mongol National Organisation and the Jana Jati Party, but the persons involved were mostly Kiratas. It is also alleged that the Kirat Yakthung Chumlung of Kathmandu is a fraternal organisation of the United Marxist–Leninist (UML) Party whereas the Kirat Yakthung Songchumbo is pro-Nepali Congress (NC). The national or regional political parties cannot really be isolated from such cultural/ethnic organisations for the leaders as also the supporters are often the same individuals and groups.

The political parties have not only infilterated into such organisations and created factions within or between them, but they have also not spared educational institutions. In Yangnam, conflicts and clashes in the village led to the closure of the local Madhyamik School. The clash was between the supporters, who were, incidentally, all Limbus, of the Nepali Congress on the one hand and Rastriya Prajatantra Party (RPP) and UML on the other. This conflict was not confined to the village but had percolated down to the family level. In one family, the father was an NC supporter and his sons were UML supporters.

Elsewhere, in Chhinamakhu and Madi Mulkharka, the roots of factionalism were no different. Everywhere, the ruling party gradually becomes arrogant and turns a blind eye to the woes of the supporters of the other party. The distinction between party and government is, however, not always maintained even in a state like West Bengal. But there are certain established procedures for seeking redressal, though often too circuitous or expensive. In Nepal, such options simply do not exist. When the state becomes too pervasive without adequate resources for overall development, the people – Kirata or not – are affected and angry.

In this context, it may also be worthwhile to remember that there are innumerable ex-soldiers among the non-Tagadhari communities and very often they are in the forefront of these organisations. This seems to have given them an exaggerated sense of confidence, which, they imagine, can match that of the state. But they do not seem to realise that strength without legitimacy is impotent unless they can throw away the very concept of a state. This is as yet unimaginable, at least in Nepal where King Mahendra Bir Bikram Shah is still considered by many as an incarnation of Vishnu. Even in India, only a handful of scholars have started questioning the legitimacy of the state. Thus, it will perhaps take a long time before the concept of king or state can be done away with. Had it been only the state this might have been easier to accomplish but it has, behind it, a very powerful discourse which has made perceptible inroads into the Kirata psyche and being more intangible than the state, is more difficult to destroy than the state itself.

9

Whither Kiratas?

It is necessary, in the conclusion, to throw light on the trend, if any, in Kirata politics. This necessitates a careful weighing of the choices available and an estimation of their mood(s) as well. Yet the prediction of the future, even when based on a sound assessment of the past and the present situations, becomes a matter of chance and hence fallible.

In recapitulating the past, one may begin with a period from which authentic historical documents are available. This period begins in the mid-seventeenth century in Sikkim, which then included the present district of Darjeeling, and in the late eighteenth century in Nepal. Though Kirata history prior to these dates is not very clear, available literature shows that their general degeneration began after that. In Sikkim, Bhutia hegemony was responsible for their decline whereas in Nepal it was the Tagadharis who systematically marginalised the subjugated peoples including the Kiratas there. And both Sikkim and Nepal were backed by strong and all-pervasive Buddhist and Hindu discourses sapping the very morale of the 'animistic' communities living there.

The Kiratas probably would not have suffered as much as they did without certain other historical events. The royal matrimony between the Limbus and the Bhutias, reinforced by the enactment of the 'blood' treaty called Lhomentsongsum, not only neutralised the Limbus but also the Lepchas of Sikkim. Similarly, the induction of Brahman priests in the Kirata royal households in east Nepal sowed the germs of the latter's ultimate downfall. Such priests were instrumental in ensuring the victory of the Tagadharis over the Kirata rulers there.

Once the Bhutia rule in Sikkim and the Gorkha rule in Nepal were established, things began to change for the worse for the indigenous peoples. Soon they began to lose their traditional identities and became parts of larger entities—Buddhist or Hindu. But the indigenous peoples could hardly voice their dissent under the hereditary, theocratic monarchs in both Sikkim and Nepal. Such a revolt would have been immediately subdued unless the person(s) concerned could flee their countries of origin and take asylum somewhere else. Moreover, there were hardly any educational and employment opportunities in these kingdoms. All this made the Kiratas and other subjugated peoples migrate to neighbouring countries and regions. Those who stayed behind became minorities in their own homelands.

The end result of such processes was what Stavenhagen has called "ethnocide" (1987:74–75). This is first characterised by the gradual alienation of land from Kiratas to Tagadharis and other categories through discriminatory legislative, administrative and judicial measures adopted by the Gorkha rulers in Nepal. The same was true for the Lepchas and Limbus under the Namgyals in Sikkim. Ethnocide for the Kiratas and Lepchas also meant the almost total replacement of their traditional values, beliefs, festivals, rituals and even language. Though a few of them were somehow successful in protecting their culture and language, the overall impact was devastating. No other concept could, perhaps, supersede 'ethnocide' as a description of what happened to the Kiratas and other such peoples in the eastern Himalayas.

One might like to pause here and ask: What has happened to the Tagadhari migrants? To be true, they were considerably deHinduised and this is evident from the low status assigned to those Tagadharis who live in east Nepal and Sikkim or Darjeeling by their counterparts in west Nepal. The migrant Tagadharis are believed to have acquired a lot of non-Brahmanical food habits and manners. The erosion of Brahmanical traits among the eastern Bahuns is alleged to be so great that the western Bahuns hesitate to give their daughters in marriage to them. This is, however, quite natural for a migrant people. The Mangars and Gurungs who migrated to east Nepal have a similar problem of acquiring girls from west Nepal.

The Bhutias in Sikkim are also migrants from Bhutan and Tibet but they did not have to shed their traditions and culture after settling in Sikkim. Whereas the state has proved to be a destroyer of the local culture, it has also served as the protector of the migrant culture. The Bhutia success was, however, possible also because they were primarily concentrated in north Sikkim, which was inaccessible to outsiders during the British period. For strategic reasons this area is largely inaccessible even today. Further, one should remember that Sikkim was also a smaller Himalayan kingdom than Nepal.

The Hinduisation of the Kiratas is definitely a much more powerful and pervading process than the deHinduisation of the Tagadharis. This is not surprising when the very state and its official discourse sought to strengthen the process as it was necessary for nation-building in Nepal. The Kirata voice was never strong enough to challenge such domination. Many chose to escape by migrating, little realising that the Tagadhari discourse embraced them wherever they settled.

The 'merger' of Sikkim with India in 1975 and the ushering in of democracy in Nepal after a bloody revolution in 1990, however, gave a lot of respite to such marginalised nationalities. Subsequently, there has been a world-wide awareness of the rights and cultures of indigenous peoples. These developments opened the floodgates for ethnic/cultural resurgence of such peoples in Sikkim as well as in Nepal.

The salient features of Kirata politics in the region may be summarised thus. One, they are trying to reinvent their traditions for which they are resorting to their oral traditions. Two, they are trying to spread a sense of cultural consciousness amongst themselves, which essentially includes the tenuous task of separating those cultural traits which they consider to be their 'own' from those which they believe to be of Aryan origin. Finally, they are seeking various kinds of social reforms, including political reform, so that their culture, language and religion can grow in a climate free from intimidation or humiliation.

It may be noted that the Kiratas are reinventing their traditions not only at the level of the respective communities but also at the racial (Mongoloid), social (Janajati) or national (Kirata) levels. However, as of now, the Limbu, Khambu or Yakkha identities are of more interest than the larger, more abstract, identities like Kirata, Mongoloid and Janajati. Kirata nationalism is still nascent with no clear indication of its maturing fully in the immediate future. Many so-called Kirata organisations are essentially Limbu organisations. Hence, the word 'Kirata' has not emerged fully as a symbol of unity within, or difference without, in the region under study.

There is another development which is taking place at a fast pace in east Nepal whereas in Darjeeling and Sikkim it has been around for some time. This is the process of conversion to Christianity. This is happening more as a protest against Tagadhari (Hindu) hegemony than anything else. "What place do we have in the Hindu society? Unless we discard the Hindu religion we cannot discard the Tagadharis," remarked a newly converted Limbu of Sankhuwa Sabha district. The phenomenon of proselytisation cannot have such simplistic answers but the disenchantment with Hinduism and its trappings could well have contributed to it.

Fanon's theory of the 'cycle of ideological interaction' between the dominant and dominated races (1967:38–44) speaks of three stages of such interaction. The first stage is characterised by the acceptance by the dominated races of the devaluation of their race and culture; the second stage is marked by the dominated races' assertion of their language, culture and religion; and the third stage shows their decision to fight all forms of subjugation, domination and exploitation by the former race.

Kirata politics in the eastern Himalayas may be viewed as representing a threshold situation which is characterised by a gradual transition from Fanon's stage one to stage two. Whereas a large majority of them still accept the devaluation of their races and cultures, some have begun asserting the importance of their own language, culture and religion. Yet they are far from graduating to the third stage. In other words, their nationalism bears characteristics of what Clifford Geertz calls the "formative stage of nationalism", which consists essentially of:

> confronting the dense assemblage of cultural, racial, local, and linguistic categories of self-identification and social loyalty that centuries of an instructed history had produced with a simple, abstract, deliberately constructed, and almost painfully self-conscious concept of political ethnicity —a proper "nationality" in the modern manner (1975:239).

One sure problem in overcoming Geertz's formative stage of nationalism is the existence of multiple boundaries. The Kiratas were aware of this prior to the post-structuralist revelation of multiple frames. These are not only overlapping but also intermeshed. The Kiratas, for instance, are not just Kiratas but also Mongols, Janajatis, Paharis, Nepalis, Gorkhalis, and so on, besides being Limbus, Khambus or Yakkhas as the case may be. Further, they are peasants, landlords, tenants, besides being members of various clans, villages, political parties and religious denominations. Finally, there are strong regional/local groupings like Darjeelinge, Kalimponge, Sikkime, Ilamme, Panchthare, Terethume, Bhojpure and so on. Such multiple identities have been responsible for delaying the process of nation-formation. Unless the leaders can hold the masses to some consciously chosen boundaries, and not let them break out—by no means an easy task—the scenario of Kirata politics may not change much in the near future.

This depends partly on how the state or the surrogate state responds to Kirata politics. As Leo Kuper writes, "there may be greater racial discrimination in reaction to a perceived threat as members of the subordinate race acquire the culture of the dominant group" (1974:28). Such discrimination is more likely in Nepal for Tagadhari interests are more strongly guarded there. The Tagadhari reaction in the post-Janajati era has been basically 'intellectual'—trying to argue through the media and other publications that non-Tagadhari politics is not in the national interest of Nepal. Of course, they are also coming together in an organised form, and share a strong sense of a 'perceived threat'. If this perception of a threat makes them respond the way Kuper writes, the task of the non-Tagadhari leaders will be much easier.

The escalation or non-escalation of the non-Tagadhari movement in Nepal depends to a great extent on the wisdom of the Tagadharis. What the latter have to reconcile with is the fact that they can no longer afford to have the power and privileges they did earlier under the hereditary rulers. They will have to forgo many of their age-old privileges not only to their non-Tagadhari countrymen but also to their own underprivileged fellow caste members in remote villages. Unless there is more sharing of the limited state resources across castes, communities and classes, movements of one type or another are bound to grow.

Working on the Gorkhaland Movement in Darjeeling (1992) showed me that parting with power and privileges is easier said than done. That is one reason why the transfer of power is more often than not accompanied by violence. Violence is also increasingly acknowledged to be the most effective language for communicating with the state which seldom understands the language of memoranda, poetry, art, theatre, pamphlets, processions or pure reason. And violence is always followed by counter-violence, normally much more violent as it destroys human dignity itself.

The redressals sought by various Kirata or allied organisations in the region are incidentally within the nation-state framework. Most such organisations would be satisfied with some kind of constitutional safeguards as those that exist in India for the scheduled castes, tribes and backward classes. Only one organisation has been seeking some sort of federalism which, however, comes down to the same thing, that is, a more equitable distribution of power and resources among communities and regions.

It is not difficult to understand why such demands are not conceded by the state and why it chooses to crush such movements by branding them anti-national or separatist. It is also not difficult to understand why the aspirations of such marginalised nationalities remain choked until they sacrifice their life and blood. It is always the state which decides what is just and legitimate and what is not, and every state has its own stake in patronising the dominant community.

A Select Bibliography

Aaloke. 1988. "Purbanchalma Limbuwan Swatantra Rajyako Nara". 20 (29).

Acharya, Baburam. 1966. *Nepalko Samkshipta Vritanta*. Kathmandu: Pramod Samsher and Nir Bikram 'Pyasi'.

Adhikari, Krishna Kant. 1984. *Nepal under Jung Bahadur 1846–1877*. Kathmandu: Sahayogi Press.

Allen, Nick J. 1976. Studies in the Myths and Oral Traditions of the Thulung Rai of East Nepal. Ph.D. thesis, Oxford University.

———. 1987. "Thulung Weddings: The Hinduisation of a Ritual Cycle in East Nepal". *L'Ethnographie*, LXXXIII, 15–33.

Anderson, Benedict. 1991. *Imagined Communities: Reflections on the Origin and Spread of Nationalism*. London: Verso.

Appadurai, Arjun. 1988. "Introduction: Place and Voice in Anthropological Theory". *Cultural Anthropology*, 3 (1), 16–20.

Arya, Gambhir Rai. 1980. *Hindu Dharma, Kirant Jati ra Eshai Mat*. Kalimpong: Himalayan Observer.

Aryal, D., R. Regmi, and **N. Rimal** (eds). 1982. *Nepal District Profile: A Districtwise Socio-Techno-Economic Profile of Nepal*. Kathmandu: National Research Associates.

Aryal, Rishi Ram. 1985. *Majh Kirat*. Bhojpur: Triveni Press.

Bagchi, G. C. 1972. *Village Survey Monograph on Upper Pedong*. Census of India, 1961. Calcutta: Government of India Press.

Bandhu, Chuda Mani. 1989. "The Role of the Nepali Language in Establishing the National Unity and Identity in Nepal". *Kailash*, 15 (3 & 4), 721–34.

Barth, Fredrik. 1969. *Ethnic Groups and Boundaries*. Boston: Little Brown & Co.

Barnouw, Victor. 1955. "Eastern Nepalese Marriage Customs and Kinship Organisation". *Southwestern Journal of Anthropology*, 11, 15–30.

Bauman, Zygmut. 1973. *Culture as Praxis*. London: Routledge & Kegan Paul.

Baxter, P. T. W. 1993. "The Creation and Constitution of Oromo Nationality". *Nordic Researcher Training Course on Ethnicity and Nationalism: Historical and Anthropological Approaches*. Sandbjer Manor (23–29 May).

Bhandari, Krishna Prasad. 1959. "Pallokiratko Zagga". *Samyukta Prayas*, August 30.

Bista, D. B. 1980. *People of Nepal*. Kathmandu: Ratna Pustak Bhandar.

———. 1991. *Fatalism and Development: Nepal's Struggle for Modernization*. Hyderabad: Orient Longman.

Boehm, M. H. 1933. "Nationalism". *Encyclopaedia of the Social Sciences*, Vol II. New York: Macmillan.

Brass, Paul R. 1985. "Ethnic Groups and the State". Paul R. Brass (ed), *Ethnic Groups and the State*. London: Croom Helm.

Burton, F. and **Pat Carlen.** 1979. *Official Discourse: On Discourse Analysis, Government Publication, Ideology and the State*. London: Routledge & Kegan Paul.

Campbell, C. A. 1845. *The Darjeeling Guide Including a Description of the Country, and of its Climate, Soil and Production*. Calcutta: Samuel Smith & Co.

Caplan, Lionel. 1967. "Some Political Consequences of State Land Policy in East Nepal". *Man*, 2 (1).

———. 1970. *Land and Social Change in East Nepal: A Study of Hindu–Tribal Relations*. London: Routledge & Kegan Paul.

———. 1990. "'Tribes' in the Ethnography of Nepal: Some Comments on a Debate". *Contributions to Nepalese Studies*, 17 (2).

———. 1991. "From Tribe to Peasant? The Limbus and the Nepalese State". *The Journal of Peasant Studies*, 18 (2), 305–21.

Chatterjee, Suniti Kumar. 1951. *Kirata-Jana-Krti: The Indo-Mongoloids: Their Contribution to the History and Culture of India*. Calcutta: Royal Asiatic Society of Bengal.

Chemjong, Iman Singh. 1961. *Limbu–Nepali–Angreji Shabdakosh*. Kathmandu: Nepal Academy.

———. 1966. *History and Culture of the Kirat People*, Parts I & II. Fidim: C. H. Jabegou.

———. 1973. *Kirat Sahityako Itihas*. Terethum: Manishankar Sering Limbu.

———. 1982. *Kirat Itihas*. 3rd Edition. Varanasi: Prakash Printing Press.

Clifford, James. 1988. *The Predicament of Culture: Twentieth Century Ethnography, Literature and Art*. Cambridge: Harvard University Press.

C'wang, T. 1990. "Stirring up a Hornet's Nest". *Sikkim Observer*, September 1.

Dahal, Dharnidhar. 1984. *Sikkimko Rajnaitik Itihas*. Part I. Gangtok: Subba Prakashan.

Dahal, Dilli Ram. 1979. "Tribalism as an Incongruous Concept in Modern Nepal". M. Gaborieou and A. Thorner (eds), *Asie du Sud Traditions et Changements*. Paris: Centre de la Recherche Scientifique.

———. 1983. Poverty or Plenty: Innovative Responses to Population Pressure in an Eastern Nepalese Hill Community. Ph.D. thesis, University of Hawaii.

———. 1988. "Political Organisation and the Changing Role of Leadership: A Study of the Athpahariya Community". *Contributions to Nepalese Studies*, 15 (1), 45–106.

———. 1996. "The Fallout of Deviant Anthropology." *Himal*, May.

Dahal, Mahesh Raj. 1990. "Sanskar-Sanskriti-Sandarva Yakkha Jatiko". *Himali Bela*, August 15–21.

Dalton, Edward Tuite. 1872. *Descriptive Ethnology of Bengal*. Calcutta: Office of the Superintendant of Government Printing.

Danda, A. K. 1988. "Tribe in India". *Man in India*, 68 (4), 313–34.

———. 1992. "The Aryan Identity: An Anthropological Approach". *Journal of the Indian Anthropological Society*, 27, 78–84.

Dash, Arthur Jules. 1947. *Bengal District Gazetteers: Darjeeling*. Alipore: Bengal Government Press.

Devalle, Susana B. C. 1992. *Discourses of Ethnicity: Culture and Protest in Jharkhand*. New Delhi: Sage Publications.

District Statistical Handbook: Darjeeling. 1971, Series 22, West Bengal, Part X A & B. Calcutta: Superintendant of Government Printing.

Driem, George Louis van. 1987. A Grammar of Limbu. Ph.D. thesis, University of Leiden.

Erdman, Howard L. 1979. "Autonomy Movements in India". Raymond L. Hall (ed), *Ethnic Autonomy: Comparative Dynamics: The Americas, Europe and the Developing World*. New York: Pergamon Press.

English, Richard. 1983. Gorkhali and Kiranti: Political Economy in the Eastern Hills of Nepal. Ph.D. thesis, New School for Social Research, New York.

Fanon, Franz. 1967. *The Wretched of the Earth*. Harmondsworth: Penguin.

Firth, Raymond. 1954. "Social Organisation and Social Change". *The Journal of the Royal Anthropological Institute of Great Britain and Ireland*, 84, 1–20.

Fisher, William F. 1993. "Nationalism and the Janajati". *Himal*, March/April 11–14.

Foucault, Michel. 1980. *Power/Knowledge: Selected Interviews and Other Writings 1972–77*. New York: Random House.

Fox, Richard G. (ed). 1990. *Nationalist Ideologies and the Production of National Cultures*. Washington: American Anthropological Association.

Fox, Robin. 1976. *Kinship and Marriage*. Harmondsworth: Penguin.

Gaenszle, Martin. 1993. "Interactions of an Oral Tradition: Changes in the *Muddum* of the Mewahang Rai of East Nepal". G. Toffin (ed), *Nepal, Past and Present*. New Delhi: Sterling.

Gaige, F. H. 1975. *Regionalism and National Unity in Nepal*. London: University of California Press.

Gates, Jr H. L. 1986. "Editor's Introduction: Writing 'Race' and the Difference it Makes" H. L. Gates, Jr. (ed), *"Race", Writing, and Difference*. Chicago: Chicago University Press.

Geertz, Clifford. 1975. *The Interpretation of Cultures*. London: Hutchinson & Co.

Gellner, Ernest. 1987. *Nations and Nationalism*. New York: Cornell University Press.

Gramsci, A. 1996. *Selections from the Prison Notebooks*. (ed) Quentin Hoare and Geoffrey Nowell Smith. Madras: Orient Longman. Originally published 1971: London: Lawrence and Wishart.

Gurung, Gopal. 1985/1988. *Nepali Rajnitima Adekha Saehai*. Kathmandu: Author.

Gurung, Harka. 1992. "Representing an Ethnic Mosaic". *Himal*, 5 (3).

Hall, Raymond L. 1979. *Ethnic Autonomy: Comparative Dynamics: The Americas, Europe and the Developing World*. New York: Pergamon Press.

Hamilton, Francis Buchanan. 1819/1971. *An Account of the Kingdom of Nepal*. New Delhi: Manjushri.

Hanpon, Gerd. 1991. *The Rais of Eastern Nepal: Ethnic and Linguistic Grouping: Findings of the Linguistic Survey of Nepal*. Kathmandu: Linguistic Society of Nepal and Centre for Nepal and Asian Studies.

Hasrat, B. J. (ed). 1970. *History of Nepal*. Hoshiarpur: V. V. Research Institute Press.

Hermanns, Fr M. 1954. *The Indo-Tibetan: The Indo-Tibetan and Mongoloid Problem in the Southern Himalaya and North-Northeast India*. Bombay: K. L. Fernandes.

Herzfeld, Michael. 1986. "Of Definitions and Boundaries: The Status of Culture in the Culture of the State". Phyllis P. Chock and June R. Wyman (eds), *Discourse and the Social Life of Meaning*. London: Smithsonian Institution Press.

Himali Bela. 1990. "Lho-Men-Chong-Sum". Editorial, July 19–25.

Hobsbawm, E. 1984. "Introduction: Inventing Traditions". E. Hobsbawm and T. Ranger (eds), *The Invention of Tradition*. Cambridge: Cambridge University Press, 1–14.

Hodgson, Brian H. 1858. "On the Kiranti Tribe of the Central Himalaya". *Journal of the Asiatic Society*, 27 (5), 446–56.

Hooker, J. D. 1891. *Himalayan Journals*. London: Wardlock Bowden.

Hutt, Michael. 1986. "Diversity and Change in the Languages of Highland Nepal". *Contributions to Nepalese Studies*, 14 (1).

Hutt, Michael. 1991. "The 1991 Parliamentary Elections in Nepal: Political Freedom and Stability". *Asian Survey*, 31 (11), 1020–39.

Inden, Ronald. 1986. "Orientalist Reconstructions of India". *Modern Asian Studies*, 20 (3), 401–46.

India Office Library Collections. 1786–95. *Miscellaneous Manuscripts of Col. W Kirkpatrick, etc.* MSS Eur F 228/36.

———. 1852. X/1280/I.

———. 1892. *Bengal Revenue Proceedings*. P. 4099, LR No 26–27.

———. n.d. *A. J. Hopkinson Collection*. MSS Eur D. 998/20.

———. 1900. *Printed Circulars, Notes and Memoranda on Caste and Religion in Bengal, July 1900–June 1911*. MSS Eur E 295/11.

———. 1957. *Limbu Books in the Kiranti Script*. MSS Eur D 537, File No L 20/57 in Brian Hodgson Collections.

———. 1961. *Limbu History*. MSS Eur D 537.

———. 1973. *Kinship and Marriage among the Limbu of Eastern Nepal*. Ph.D. thesis, University of California.

Jones, R. and **Shirley Jones.** 1976. *The Himalayan Woman: A Study of Limbu Women in Marriage and Divorce*. Palto Alto: Mayfield Publishing.

Joshi, Hari Ram. 1985. "The Kirata Tribes". *Rolamba*, 5 (3), 21–29.

Kainla, Bairagi. 1990. *Mahaguru Phalgunandaka Upadeshharu tatha Satyehangma Panthaka Bhajanmala*. Bhadrapur: Siddhanta Chapakhana.

———. 1992. "Kirant Lipi arthat Sirijanga Lipi: Choto Charcha". *Kairan*, April/May, 16–19.

Kainla, Birahi. 1990. "Limbuko Dharmik Jiwan". *Himali Bela*, July 5–11.

———. 1992. "Limbu Bhashama Siksha ra Limbu Bhashaka Shikshak-Shikshikaharu". *Kairan*, July/August, 23–25.

Kandangwa, Kajiman. 1990. "Bhasha, Sahitya ra Sanskriti: Niti, Siddhanta ra Pratikriya —Nepalko Sandarbhama". Pamphlet, n.p.

Kirkpatrick, William. 1811/1986. *An Account of the Kingdom of Nepal: A Mission to that Country in the Year 1793*. New Delhi: Asian Educational Services.

Kohn, Hans. 1968. "Nationalism". *International Encyclopaedia of the Social Sciences*, Vol 11.

Kongpee. 1982. "Kiranti Dharma tatha Sahitya Utthan Sangh". 3 (1), 1–2, 15–24.

Kothari, Rajni. 1988. *Rethinking Development: In Search of Humane Alternatives*. Delhi: Ajanta Publications.

Koyu, C. 1992. "Kiranti Mahan Parva Sakkewako Choto Parichay". *Lenmuk*, 1 (7).

Kuper, Leo. 1974. *Race, Class, and Power*. London: Duckworth.

Laitin, David D. 1977. *Hegemony and Culture: Politics and Religious Change Among the Yoruba*. Chicago: University of Chicago Press.

Landon, Perceval. 1928/1976. *Nepal*. Vols I & II. Kathmandu: Ratna Pustak Bhandar.

Leach, E. R. 1954. *Political Systems of Highland Burma: A Study of Kachin Social Structure*. Cambridge: Harvard University Press.

Limbu, Dhan Bahadur. 1989. *Kirat Parampara Limbu Riti Thiti ra Sanskriti*. Mirik: Kirant Chumlung Sabha.

Macfarlane, Alan. 1993. "Fatalism and Development in Nepal". M. Hutt (ed), *Nepal in the Nineties: Versions of the Past, Visions of the Future*. Delhi: Oxford University Press.

Madan, T. N. 1962. "Is the Brahmanic *Gotra* a Grouping of Kin?". *Southwestern Journal of Anthropology*, 18, 59–77.

Magar, Pradip. 1992. "Bhasik Andolanko Awashyakta Kina?". *Kairan*, 1 (6), 20–21.

Manen, Prem Nath. 1984. "Limbu (Kirat) Bhasha-Sahitya bare". *Sambardhan*, 1 (2), 59–65.

McDougal, Charles. 1973. "Structure and Division in Kulunge Rai Society". *Kailash*, 1 (3), 205–24.

———. 1979. *The Kulunge Rai: A Study in Kinship and Marriage Exchange*. Kathmandu: Ratna Pustak Bhandar.

Michailovsky, Boyd. 1975. "Notes on the Kiranti Verb (East Nepal)". *Linguistics of the Tibeto-Burman Area*, 2 (2), 183–218.

Mishra, K. C. 1987. *The Tribes in the Mahabharata*. New Delhi: National Book House.

Morris, John. 1933/1985. *The Gurkhas: An Ethnology*. Delhi: B. R. Publications.

Namgyal, Thutob and **Maharani Yeshi Drolma.** 1908. *History of Sikkim*. Gangtok: typescript.

Nandy, Ashis. 1997. "State". Wolfgang Sachs (ed), *The Development Dictionary: A Guide to Knowledge and Power*. New Delhi: Orient Longman. Originally published 1992: London: Zed Books.

Naba Pravah. 1991. 1 (23).

Nembhang, Bir. 1990. "Nepalko Bhavi Sambidhanma Limbuwan Swayattako Pravdhan Hunuparcha". *Mechi Pravah*, 8 (20).

———. 1991. "Gopal Gurungko Aarop kati Satya, kati Asatya?". Pamphlet.

———. 1992. "Limbu Sanskritika kehi Biseshtaharu". *Kairan*, January/Feburary, 8–9.

Nepal District Profile: A Districtwise Socio-Techno-Economic Profile of Nepal. 1982. (ed) Aryal, R.Regmi and N. Rimal. Kathmandu: National Research Associates.

Nepal, N. 1988. "Prachin Nepal Upatyakaka Kirantharu". *Current Nepal*, 4 (7 & 8), 1–14.

Nepali, Gopal Singh. 1965. *The Newars: An Ethno-Sociological Study of a Himalayan Community*. Bombay: Asia.

Northey, W. M. and **J. Morris.** 1974. *The Gurkhas: Their Manners, Customs and Country*. Delhi: Cosmo Publications.

Okada, Ferdinand E. 1957. "Ritual Brotherhood: A Cohesive Factor in Nepalese Society". *Southwestern Journal of Anthropology*, 13 (3), 212–22.

O'Malley, L. S. S. 1907. *Bengal District Gazetteers: Darjeeling*. Alipore: Bengal Government Press.

Pahari, Anup. 1992. "Fatal Myth: A Critique of Fatalism and Development". *Himal*, January/February, 52–54.

Parasher, Aloka. 1991. *Mlecchas in Early India: A Study in Attitudes towards Outsiders upto AD 600*. New Delhi: Munshiram Manoharlal.

Phadnis, Urmila. 1990. *Ethnicity and Nation Building in South Asia*. New Delhi: Sage.

Plank, P. H. van der. 1975. "Language and Nationalism: A Historical Review on the Role of Language in Nationalistic Ideologies". *Plural Societies*, 6 (3), 9–15.

Po'dar, Prem and **T. B. Subba.** 1991. "Demystifying Some Ethnographic Texts on the Himalayas". *Social Scientist*, 19 (8–9), 78–84.

Pradhan, Kumar. 1991. *The Gorkha Conquests: The Process and Consequences of the Unification of Nepal, with Particular Reference to Eastern Nepal*. Calcutta: Oxford University Press.

Pradhan, Paras Mani. 1978. "Nepal". *The Cultural Heritage of India*, Vol 5.

Prapannacharya, Swami. 1981. *Vedma ke Chha?*. Prayag: Chirinjivi Dharma.

Prindle, Peter H. 1975. "Fictive Kinship (*mit*) in East Nepal". *Anthropos*, 70, 877–82.

Raftopoulos, Brian. 1993. "Zimbabeve: Race and Nationalism in a Post Colonial State". *Nordic Research Training Course on Ethnicity and Nationalism: Historical and Anthropological Approaches*. Sandbjerg Manor (23–29 May).

Rai, D. 1991. *Nepalko Janajati Bareka kehi Kuraharu*. Mirong: S. D. Songoni.

Rai, Ganga Raj. 1992. "Kirat Rai Yayokkhako Choto Chinari". *Yayok*, 1–4.

Rai, Naval Kishore. 1992. "Rai (Khambu) Bhashaharuko Vikas Garne Jamarko Garda". *Yayok*, 5–11.

Rai, S. K. 1991. "Kirat Mundhum Dharma: Ek Samchipta Charcha". *Kairan*, November/December.

Rai, Tirtha Raj Mukarung. 1992. *Raika Pachhaharu, Sainoka Bhashaharu*. Dilpa: Mukarung Prakashan.

Redfield, Robert. 1956. *Peasant Society and Culture*. Chicago: University of Chicago Press.

Regmi, D. R. 1969. *Ancient Nepal*. 3rd Edition. Calcutta: Firma KLM.

Regmi, Mahesh C. 1976a. *Landownership in Nepal*. London: University of California Press.

———. 1976b. "Some Questions on Nepali History". *Contributions to Nepalese Studies*, 3 (2), 1–5.

Regmi Research Collections. 1974. 6 (5 & 9).

———. 1990. 2 (12).

Risley, H. H. 1891/1981. *The Tribes and Castes of Bengal*. Vol II. Calcutta: Firma KLM.

———. 1915/1969. *The People of India*. Delhi: Oriental.

———. 1972. *The Gazetteer of Sikkim*. New Delhi: Manjushri.

Risley, H. H., George Grierson and **William Crooke.** 1931/1975. *The Ethnology, Language, Literature and Religions of India*. Delhi: The Academic Press.

Rose, Leo E. and **Margaret W. Fisher.** 1970. *The Politics of Nepal: Persistence and Change in an Asian Monarchy*. Ithaca: Cornell University Press.

Rothchild, D. 1986. "Hegemonial Exchange: An Alternative Model for Managing Conflict in Middle Africa". Dennis L. Thompson and Dov Ronen (eds), *Ethnicity, Politics and Development*. Boulder: Lynne Rienner Publishers, 65–104.

Russell, Andrew. 1992. The Yakha: Culture, Environment and Development in East Nepal. Ph.D. thesis, Oxford University.

———. 1994. "Traditions in Transition: Sanskritization and Yakhafication in East Nepal". Durham–Paris Conference on *The Invention and Re-Invention of Tradition*.

Said, Edward W. 1978. *Orientalism*. Harmondsworth: Penguin.

Sangma, Milton S. 1985. "The Kiratas in Indian Literature". *Journal of NEICSSR*, 9 (1), 56–59.

Sanyal, Charu Chandra. 1979. *The Limbus: A South Eastern Himalayan Kirata People*. Calcutta: Dipti Printing.

Seddon, David, William Blaikie and **James Cameron.** 1979. *Peasants and Workers in Nepal*. New Delhi: Vikas.

———. 1980. *Nepal in Crisis: Growth and Stagnation at the Periphery*. Delhi: Oxford University Press.

———. 1984. *Nepal, A State of Poverty: The Political Economy of Population Growth and Social Deprivation*. Norwich: Monographs in Development Studies No 11, University of East Anglia.

Sengupta, Sunil. n.d. "Multilingualism and Multilingual Communication Field in East and North-Eastern Himalayan Region". Centre for Himalayan Studies, Special Lecture No XI.

Shaha, Rishikesh. 1975. *Nepali Politics: Retrospect and Prospect*. Delhi: Oxford University Press.

Sharma, Janaklal. 1982. *Hamro Samaj: Ek Adhyayan*. Kathmandu: Sajha Prakashan.

Sharma, Prayag Raj. 1978. "Nepal: Hindu–Tribal Interface". *Contributions to Nepalese Studies*, 13 (2), 130–35.

———. 1986. "Ethnicity and National Integration in Nepal: A Statement of the Problem". *Contributions to Nepalese Studies*, 13 (2), 130–35.

Shrestha, S. K. 1985. *Limbuwanko Aitihasik Adhyayan*. Kathmandu Srijana Printers.

Shrestha, T. N. 1989. *Nepalese Administration: A Historical Perspective*. Kathmandu: Rhino Publications.

Sikkim at a Glance. 1981. Gangtok: Bureau of Economics and Statistics, Government of Sikkim.

Sikkim Observer. 1987. "Limbus of Sikkim -I: Lhomentsongsum". 1 (31).

———. 1987. "Limbus: A Neglected Lot". July 11–17, 25–31.

———. 1987. "Letters Relating to Demand for Scheduled Tribe Status by Limbus of Sikkim". August 8–14.

———. 1988. "Lho-Men-Tsong-Sum Unity revived". October 24–November 5.

———. 1989. "Demand for Autonomy Raised". May 6.

———. 1990. "Limbus Demand ST Status". July 14.

———. 1990. "Limbus for Distinct Identity". July 21.

———. 1990. "Limbu Memorandum to the President (Full Text of the Document)". July 28.

———. 1990. "Nepali, Gorkhali and Now Kiranti". August 25.

———. 1990. "Chumlung Demands CM's Resignation". November 24.

———. 1990. "Govt rejects Mandal Report". September 8.

———. 1991. "Chumlung for Reservation of Tsong Seat". February 29

———. 1991. "Limbus, Tamangs to be Made Scheduled Tribes". October 28.

Singh, G. P. 1990. *The Kiratas in Ancient India*. New Delhi: Gian Publishing House.

Sinha, A. C. 1975. *Politics of Sikkim: A Sociological Study*. Faridabad: Thompson Press.

———. 1983. *Studies in the Himalayan Communities: Text and Context*. New Delhi: Books Today.

Smith, M. G. 1993. "Race and Ethnicity". Ralph Premdas (ed), *The Enigma of Ethnicity: An Analysis of Race in the Caribbean and the World*. Trinidad: The University of the West Indies.

Snyder, Louis L. 1982. *Global Mini-Nationalisms: Autonomy or Independence*. Westport: Greenwood Press.

Songpangphe, Rishi Kumar. 1992. *Yakthung Chokthim*. Kalimpong: Kiranti Prakashan.

Spencer, Jonathan. 1990. "Writing Within: Anthropology, Nationalism, and Culture in Sri Lanka". *Current Anthropology*, 31 (3), 283–300.

Stavenhagen, R. 1987. "Ethnocide or Ethnodevelopment: The New Challenge". *Development: Seeds of Change*, 1, 74–78.

Stiller, Ludwig F. 1973/1975. *The Rise of the House of Gurkha: A Study in the Unification of Nepal 1768–1816*. Ranchi: The Patna Jesuit Society.

Subba, Aasman. 1988. *Kiratiya Dharma ra Karma Sanskar*. Kathmandu: Akshar Chapakhana.

Subba, T. B. 1985a. "Caste Relations in Nepal and India". *Social Change*, 15 (4), 23–26.

———. 1985b. *The Quiet Hills: A Study of Agrarian Relations in Hill Darjeeling*. Delhi: ISPCK.

———. 1989. *Dynamics of a Hill Society: The Nepalis in Darjeeling and Sikkim Himalayas*. Delhi: Mittal Publications.

———. 1992. *Ethnicity, State and Development: A Case Study of Gorkhaland Movement in Darjeeling*. New Delhi: Vikas.

Symonolewics, K. S. 1965. "Nationalist Movements: An Attempt at a Comparative Typology". *Comparative Studies in Society and History*, 7 (2), 221–30.

Tamang, Sitaram. 1991. "Nepalma Janajati Samasya ra Samadhan". *Chahara Saptahik*, January 13.

Tathyank Gatibidhi. Volume 5, Number 2, 1983–84. Kathmandu: National Planning Commission Secretariat.

Thulung, Narad Muni. 1985. *Kiratko Nali-Beli*. Varanasi: P. P. Press.

Toba, Sueyoshi. 1992. *Rites of Passage: An Aspect of Rai Culture* Kathmandu: Royal Nepal Academy.

Upreti, B. P. 1975. *Nature and Change in Ethnic Relationships in Limbuan*. Ph.D. thesis, University of Wisconsin.

———. 1976. "Limbuwan Today: Process and Problems". *Contributions to Nepalese Studies*, 3 (2), 47–70.

Vansittart, Eden. 1915. *Gurkhas*. Calcutta: Superintendant of Government Printing.

Walakhamcha, Nirdosh. 1992. *Sakkewa: Ek Parichaya*. Kathmandu: Pratibodh Printing Press.

Weidert, A. and **Bikram Subba.** 1985. *Concise Limbu Grammar and Dictionary*. Amsterdam: Lobster Publications.

Williams, C. H. 1988. "Minority Nationalist Historiography". R. J. Johnston *et al.* (eds), *Nationalism, Self-Determination and Political Geography*. New York: Croom Helm.

Wright, D. (ed). 1877/1972. *History of Nepal*. Kathmandu: Nepal Antiquated Book Publishers.

Youngya, Chandra Prasad. 1990. *Mongol Kirant: Samchipta Itihas tatha Darshan*. Jhapa: Prasad Subba.

Index